# Come Rain
# Or Come Shine

### Live, Love, Laugh
### Weep, Wail and Wonder
### Book Two

## George and Carmela
## Cunningham

© 2021 George Lee Cunningham and Carmela Cunningham.

ISBN 978-1-7323345-3-3

Reader Publishing Group
Banning CA 92220

Visit our websites at
www.readerpublishing.com
And
www.GeorgeLeeCunningham.com

For Willie

**Who Broke Our Hearts**

# Dear Reader

This is the second book in a series we call Live, Love, Laugh, Weep, Wail and Wonder – a half-dozen words that we think pretty much sum up life. These essays were written over more than two decades – even though some of the stories happened much longer ago than that. They focus on the people we've met, the people we've loved, and the things that have happened along the way.

Some essays were originally published in a newsletter we co-founded called, The Cunningham Report. Others were added later on our readerpublishing.com website, and still others are brand new.

We have had this idea of writing an essay book about life for more than 10 years. When we finally started pulling it all together, we realized that although some of our selections were light-hearted and humorous, others were more thoughtful, and even sad. They all seem to recognize that like candy, life can be either sweet or tart, and sometimes a bit of both.

The first book in this two-part series is called "On the Sunny Side of the Street." Although these two books are not a chronology, we hope you read "Sunny Side" first, as it sets the stage for "Rain or Shine."

We think you'll see yourself in these books – either because we've told your story, or we've told a story that could be yours.

We hope you enjoy our stories.

# CONTENTS

Introduction                                Page 11

Chapter 1: Middle Age Divide                Page 13

Chapter 2: Those We Loved and Lost          Page 49

Chapter 3: Dying with Our Boots On          Page 113

Chapter 4: Magical Times
And Magical Places                          Page 161

**Don't Forget to Get
Book One Of the**

Live, Laugh, Love
Weep, Wail and Wonder
Series

# On the Sunny
# Side of the Street

***By George and Carmela
Cunningham***

# Introduction

Life is an adventure.

Things don't always go as we want, and they hardly ever happen as we expect. Life is a mix of joy and sorrow; success and failure; regret and guilt. There are the things that we could have done better, people whom we could have treated better, important decisions that we could have made better.

Life is a bumpy and treacherous road and one on which we may lose not only our way, but also who we are and who we meant to be. Sometimes it means not only finding the path back from whatever personal wilderness in which we had been wandering, but also remembering who we are and who we want to be.

If you have led a completely successful life, followed all the rules, done well in school, gotten along with your peers, married the right person, had the proper number of children, made smart investments, enjoyed your chosen career, and retired at a young enough age to bask in the sunset of your years, then good for you.

But as everybody should know, there is more to life than that.

Unless you have experienced the heartbreak of loss, felt shame over the things you did wrong, and recognized that the biggest battle we all face is the battle within ourselves between the darkness that threatens to bring us down and the kindness and forgiveness that makes us human, then your life story has been incomplete.

The personal stories we tell in Come Rain or Come Shine reflect both happiness and loss, regret and joy. These are our stories and the stories of our friends and families, and sometimes strangers we met along the way. But they are universal to humanity. Don't be surprised if you see yourself on these pages.

When it works, civilization depends on humans' ability to overcome our darker side and seek out and bask in every bit of imperfect sunlight the world affords us.

We hope you enjoy our very personal stories.

- George and Carmela Cunningham
October 27, 2021

# Chapter 1: MIDDLE AGE DIVIDE

**PREFACE:** Jay Leno once talked about how he had bought his dad a new VCR, but his dad was afraid to use it. His dad was a World War II vet who had fought Nazis and faced death and did all kinds of brave things. And now, he was afraid of the VCR. Right off the bat, that story is dated. Leno's been off the Late Show for more than a decade, and I bet most 25-year-olds don't even know what a VCR is. But you could easily change the names to make the story relevant. And that's the important thing once you get older. Being relevant.

*Carmela*

# Essays

| | |
|---|---|
| Facing Down Middle Age in a Hot Elevator | 16 |
| Is 60 Really Better than 30? | 19 |
| The Jokes on Me | 20 |
| Stranger in a Strange Land | 21 |
| Defending the Day | 23 |
| E=MC²: Cher Explains It All | 24 |
| We Hate a Lazy Pancreas | 25 |
| Ain't Nothing Like a Book | 26 |
| No Coot Like an Old Coot | 27 |
| The Never Changing Human | 28 |
| Killing Time | 29 |
| Damn Kids | 30 |
| Putting Memories to the Music | 31 |
| Sometimes It's Just TMI | 32 |
| A Do-Over Please | 33 |
| Adventures Along the Mortal Coil | 34 |
| The Reluctant Healer | 36 |
| Incident in Check-Out Line Three | 38 |
| Our Friend Grant Young | |
| And The Whole Young Family | 40 |
| Blood Still Matters | 42 |
| When Family Comes Late to the Game | 44 |
| Taking Retirement a Step at a Time | 47 |

# Facing Down Middle Age in a Hot Elevator

Carmela – May 17, 2020

In 2014, I was a year retired from UCLA where I had spent 15 years working in a high-tech organization that supported scientific research. By the time I formally retired from UCLA, I was Chief Operating Officer of both the Office of Information Technology and of the Institute of Digital Research and Education. It was about as demanding, challenging, stressful, and exciting job as I ever could have imagined. Walking away from it surprised everybody – most of all me.

A year after I left, life wasn't much less stressful. I had contracted back to UCLA for half-time work, I was doing a lot of freelance writing for an energy conservation organization, and I was working with George on Port Town – our 500-page history of the Port of Long Beach. By the end of that year, we had sold or given away all our stuff and George, Henry the Wonder Dog, and I, hit the road to be vagabonds for a year. I kept working while we drove and figured that I would keep freelancing and working remotely at UCLA indefinitely.

At one point we came back to the West Coast and rented a 400-square-foot apartment in Long Beach to work on Port Town publicity, with the idea that we'd leave again when the six-month lease was up. And then, things started happening.

My brother-in-law Willie died. My aunt, who had been in remission from cancer for so long that we forgot to stay worried, died. I needed to help my dad care for his wife, who had been diagnosed with Alzheimer's. Within the same year, my dad had to go into assisted living. And then the worst thing happened. George had a stroke. That's not all entirely in chronological order, but it all occurred within a year.

So, there I was. Scared to death about my husband. Sad for the loss of two important people in my life. Stressed from dealing with my dad and his wife. Worried about our deadlines and our finances. Living nowhere in particular. No real job. No furniture, and no household goods beyond some things that were stuffed willy-nilly into a storage unit.

And then it was my 60th birthday. August 13 in Southern California is always blazing hot. I wanted to take George to UCLA to get some Dragon software so that he could start dictating essays and the new book he was working on.

Before his stroke, George did all the driving while Henry

16

snuggled in my lap. But two weeks after his stroke, I was doing the driving. He hated it. I hated it. And Henry really hated it. Henry whined and squirmed as we jumped on the 405 and then sat on the freeway for about two hours. When we finally got to UCLA, the parking was even worse than usual due to construction. I finally found a place on the top of a building.

As the sun burned down, the three of us stood waiting for an elevator. There were dozens of students and construction workers jamming into each elevator car, and we waited for several minutes to get an empty car going down. I fretted that George and Henry were getting burned and over-heated.

Finally, an elevator car was heading down, and it was empty except for one construction worker. We got in, but before the door closed, the construction guy stuck his key in a slot and turned the elevator so it was heading back up to an elevated construction area.

"Did you just turn this elevator," I demanded.

"Yeah," the guy said.

"You stupid, fucking jackass," I yelled. "You fucking moron! I'll kill you!"

And then I turned around to see about a dozen students staring at me like I was crazy. Here is what they saw.

A 60-year-old woman with wild hair wearing a low-cut silk blouse, big dark glasses, white shorts and high-heeled sandals, pushing a baby stroller with a large Yorkie in it.

And then I burst into tears.

OK. I was 60 years old and I had no plan. We had to go to ground, so a few months later I moved us into an old-age home. Well, that's how I saw it at the time. It's actually a 55 and older gated community that has proved to be quite pleasant and easy to leave behind for months at a time as we go traveling. I moved farther away from family and friends. I moved away from the ocean and the downtown I loved. I moved away from being in the middle of a business community where George and I had some reputation. I gave up the freelance jobs and UCLA work.

I started to wonder who I was. And, I was scared. I didn't want to become an old grump. And I sure didn't want to become one of those over-made-up, way-too-short-skirted old ladies walking around saying things like, "that's effing awesome!" Mostly, I didn't want to become irrelevant. Did I say I was scared? I was petrified.

But time marches on. George made a full recovery, and we bought new furniture for our new home. I started gardening and making friends. I started volunteering at the prison and doing yoga. I took piano lessons and worked on book projects.

That's when I realized that I could make my own choices and

craft my own kind of old lady. I could find my place, picking and choosing the new technologies and music and clothes and vernacular that suited me, but also keeping the old things and ideas that make me comfortable. I began, for the first time in my life, doing the things I wanted to do, and I stopped worrying about work or success or what people thought about me. I realized they likely didn't think much about me at all. I started to look at this time of my life – my very own middle age, old middle-age, some might say – as the time to do anything I wanted to do.

And that's what I've been doing for the past half-decade – exactly what I want to do.

# Is 60 Really Better than 30?

Carmela – October 19, 2009

Have you read all those stories about how 60 is the new 40 and 30 is the new 20, and so on and so forth? Supposedly the idea is that people who are now in their 60s, are living and conducting themselves like people used to do when they were in their 40s. And people in their 30s are now living and conducting themselves like people used to do when they were in their 20s.

We don't want to be negative, but being 60 isn't like being 30 no matter how many hours you spend in the gym or popping little blue pills at bedtime. And if you're 30-something, and you're acting like you're 20-something, let's face it, you're just immature.

People may be living longer, and life indeed may have gotten better for mature citizens. We not only concede the fact, we live it. It's not just pharmaceuticals and healthy living. It's attitude too. People are no longer willing to retire to their rocking chairs when they turn 60. We want to be out on the street, kicking butts and taking names.

It's not like being in our 30s. It's better. We're still healthy and active enough to enjoy life, but we're a heck of a lot smarter than we were three decades earlier. Or at least we ought to be.

But, unlike animals, humans can do arithmetic. And just because we don't always like the answers, that doesn't change the facts. The fact is when you're in your 60s, you're not in your 30s, and you never will be again.

Still, we try to keep an open mind. Recently we saw a story in the newspaper food section that postulated that cookies are the new toast.

Now that just makes sense.

# The Joke's on Me

George – January 22, 2007

People are always saying how you're only as old as you feel, but we all know that's simply not true. When I say we, I mean we who have been around long enough to understand that God can sometimes play cruel – but often instructive – practical jokes on us.

Like when you are walking down a street, and you're having a good day, and you feel like you did when you were 30, then you happen to glance over as you pass a store window, and you're shocked at the old person looking back at you.

That just God's way of saying, be grateful for those times when you feel young and energetic and as good as you ever were, but please don't ever confuse that with reality. Unlike some television preachers, I have never had God speak directly to me, but I sure do get the message.

Being reminded of your age is more than just how you look. For instance, I went to a very nice event a few days ago, full of folks concerned about important issues. Sitting at a nearby table was a middle-aged, well-dressed gent with a bone through his nose. He seemed like a nice man, drinking a cup of coffee and chatting with the other folks at the table. And nobody even mentioned his nose bone.

I thought about just going up and asking him, excuse me, but why do you wear a bone in your nose? But the answer was obvious. He felt it was attractive, and who am I to say he is wrong? It was a very nice bone, polished and tapered, sticking out on both sides like some kind of giant cat whisker. I held my tongue, but every once in a while, I would look over at him, and be reminded that I am now a wallflower at the big dance. When I was young, nobody wore a bone in his nose, except maybe in the National Geographic. Now a nose bone is no big deal.

It didn't bother me though. I'm used to God and His practical jokes.

# Stranger in a Strange Land

George – May 27, 2013

I have this nightmare where I come from a planet, which we can call 20th Century Earth, and I crash land on a similar, but different, planet called 21st Century Earth. The inhabitants of Earth21 are the same in appearance to the Earth20 inhabitants, except the Earth21 people are all younger.

On Earth20 people communicated by talking to one another. On Earth21, the inhabitants exchange ideas and concepts by manipulating small handheld devices which send short written messages through the air – kind of like a telegraph, except without the wires and Morse code.

In my nightmare, I yearn to go back to my homeland on Earth20, but that's impossible. Once you crash land on Earth21, there is no going back. It's a one-way trip.

The real nightmare, of course, is that it's not a nightmare at all. The world I grew up in no longer exists. There are some buildings still standing, and some people from that world are still wandering around, but for the most part that world is gone forever.

We survivors of the 20th Century live in denial. Sure things have changed, we say, but that's not necessarily bad. And it's not. No matter how some of us survivors try to sugarcoat it, the 20th Century was no bed of roses. But it was our century and we felt comfortable there.

This is not our century. The aliens – which we ourselves produced – have taken over and each day their control over the planet grows stronger. This was recently illustrated to me twice in the same day.

It started with my wife complaining to me about hashtags. In case you don't know what a hashtag is, it is what we Earth20 people used to call a pound sign. It looks like this: #. We also used it as a substitute for the word "number," as in I live at "123 Main St. #201." Now it's called a hashtag and it's used when you are tweeting somebody on Twitter and you want your message to be available in a subject file.

For instance, if I tweet: "The #Dodgers is my favorite team. #MLB" then my tweet is posted on the #Dodger file along with tweets from other people who are Dodger fans and on the #MLB file along with tweets from people talking about Major League Baseball.

"I'm not doing it," my wife tells me. "I don't do hashtags or whatever silly thing they want to call the pound sign."

"Why not," I ask.

She looks at me with that stubborn look she gets, which frankly is not her best look, and tells me.

"Because, I don't want to. I don't like reading tweets with hashtags all through them, and I am certainly not going to start using hashtags myself."

"Never? You're never going to use hashtags?"

She thinks about it.

"Maybe in two or three years, I'll start using them," she says. "Maybe not. I haven't decided yet."

I absolutely understand. The poor woman is trying to stay true to the 20th Century as long as she can. I've already sold out, but not her. She is one of those people who don't forget where they came from.

Later that day, we're sitting in the Bun Boy Restaurant in Baker having lunch and she gives me that little nod of the head and eye roll that means "check this out." At a nearby table were a young man and a young woman, obviously in love, waiting for their food to be delivered. They were holding hands across the table, but they were not looking at each other. They each were using their free hand to text messages on what the Earth21 inhabitants like to call their "mobile devices."

We watched them for a while to see if we could tell whether they were texting each other or texting other people at other places in the world, but it was impossible to tell. Their faces were blank and their fingers were flying.

This is not an attack on the inhabitants of Earth21. Some of them are quite nice and very tolerant of our differences. Still, we struggle to fit in. There are people like us, people from the 20th Century, who no longer struggle, who no longer attempt to adopt the alien ways or relearn how things are done on Earth21.

They have banded together in self-created communities with names like Leisure World, Sun City and Vista Hills, where they can reminisce about the good old days without being constantly reminded that those days are gone forever.

Maybe someday I will move to a community like that, but probably not. I'm already using hashtags. I'm half-alien already. I plan to stick it out and see what happens next.

**EPILOGUE:** It's 2021 and Carmela and I live in Sun Lakes Country Club Estates. We Sun Lakers have three of our own special Sun Lakes Community Facebook pages. Hashtags abound. But Carmela doesn't use them.

# Defending the Day

George – April 17, 2006

People sometimes wonder why old people tend to be so cranky. In fact, we used to wonder about it ourselves. But one of the blessings of growing older is that we begin to understand things that used to be a mystery to us.

One reason old people tend to be cranky, is the obvious. They wake up stiff and achy every morning. And every day that goes by, it takes longer and longer for those first-thing-in-the-morning aches and pains to go away.

But the more important reason that old people get cranky is that old people can do arithmetic. For you folks who went through the public education system after about 1985, that's adding and subtracting. Old people realize that their days are limited and that they have used up a lot more of them than they have left to use. So, each one of those remaining days becomes very precious.

That's why when some rude or thoughtless person tries to ruin one of those days, old folks get a little testy about it. They talk back. They tell people off. They may even be a pain in the you-know-what. It's just their way of saying, "I've only got a limited number of days left, so don't even think of screwing this one up."

We're not saying that getting old gives a person the right to treat younger people with contempt or insult them just because they may be young and clueless. But there is such a thing as self-defense. It's like that Latin phrase that was popular a few years back. Carpe Diem. Seize the day. Cranky old folks have already seized the day.

Now they're just trying to defend it.

# E=MC²: Cher Explains it All

### Carmela – August 7, 2007

Have you noticed lately how fashionable it's become to be middle-aged? We like this a lot.

We love going online and seeing promos telling us to see the photo gallery of gorgeous women who are all over 40. We love seeing Sophia Loren and Tina Turner and Cher - all in their 50s and 60s - and still driving men wild.

We love going to movies starring Clint Eastwood and James Garner and Gene Hackman. We think they're really sexy. And, we feel somehow validated that somebody else thinks they're sexy too.

We love watching those music revues where all the really old groups - the ones from my high school days - sing the old songs one more time. A few of the guys can hit the old notes, but the ones we find most charming, are the ones who can't. They're out there singing and dancing, their pot bellies stretching their shirts, their long hair diverting your eyes from their bald spots, and their voices almost hitting the high notes.

Of course, we all know why this is happening. It's that baby boom thing again. We're reaching those years when we're supposed to be slowing down and leaving things to the next generation. But we don't want to. And because there are more of us, because we've got so much money to spend, because we're controlling the media, being 45 or 55 or even 65 is really cool.

We once heard a great quote by Cher.

"I've been 40, and I've been 50," she said. "Forty was better."

Give her a few years, she'll think 50 was swell.

**EPILOGUE:** As we go to press, Cher is 75 years old. Chastity, who now goes by Chas, is 52. Word has it, he thinks 40 was better too.

# We Hate a Lazy Pancreas

## George and Carmela – July 1, 2006

There's this guy we know, we'll call him Joe, who was complaining the other day about taking his medicine. His medicine is supposed to help his pancreas do its job.

Joe is no spring chicken, in fact he's a member of that generation that grew up during the depression, then went off to war to stop Hitler and Tojo from taking over the world. He's a tough guy, but what worries him is that if he starts babying his pancreas, it's going to get lazy and just sluff off.

Joe's not afraid to die. He just doesn't want to do it with a lazy pancreas.

We know exactly how he feels. Sometimes it's like all our organs and body parts have separate personalities. When we get ready to do something, we have to convince them all to work together and follow the leader – in this case, our brains. We're not lazy, but our parts seem to have minds of their own. Our lungs want to sit back and take it easy, our backs start whining about how stiff they are, our stomachs are gurgling and giving us gas, and our hearts are threatening to attack.

We're going to take a lesson from Joe and stop listening to all that moaning and complaining. It's time to whip those guys into shape and have them start working as a team.

Lungs, start pumping.

Back, stretch out there and limber up.

Stomach, you're going on a diet.

And heart, it's time for you to get off the bench and back in the game.

Our spirits are willing. It's just the flesh that keeps doing whatever it darn well pleases.

**EPILOGUE:** Joe managed to keep his pancreas in line for another 15 years. It finally gave out – along with the rest of his organs – in January 2021 as we were planning his 100th birthday party.

# Ain't Nothing Like a Book

## Carmela – February 20, 2006

The thing about unintended consequences is that you never see them coming. I never thought getting new carpet would change such a basic part of our lives. But it did. We have thousands of books and moving them, even for a day, is hard work. We've moved these books a dozen times, but this time is different. Between the information we can get in seconds on the Internet and the knowledge that we're never going to read McNally's Secret again, we know it's time to cut the stacks.

The books I've carried through time and space illustrate my life. Gone with the Wind, which I first read when I was 11, and a signed volume of Ulysses S. Grant's Memoirs will stay with me, as will Will and Ariel Durant's History of the World and Gibbon's Decline and Fall of the Roman Empire. The Complete Works of Shakespeare – with my 20-year-old scribblings in the margins – aren't going anywhere, and neither is the tattered set of Mark Twain from which my mother read to us The Prince and the Pauper. I'd never let go of my torn-up paperback copy of Pearl Buck's Dragonseed, but I've had it with Ayn Rand.

The Travis series stays and so does all the Vonnegut. I'm dumping Michener, but I won't part with Puzo. All the James Patterson, Patricia Cornwell and Michael Connelly go, even as I await their next offerings.

Bookcases won't be spared. Now we have oak, store-bought cases, which replaced the ones we bought unfinished and stained ourselves. Those replaced the ones we hammered together from cheap pine, which replaced the old bricks and boards. They all go. Without books, who needs the shelves?

How can we get rid of what's traveled so long and far with us? I'm not sure.

But maybe that's the real gift of books. No matter where you go or what you do, they never really leave you.

**EPILOGUE:** It's late 2020 and we've spent the last two months rearranging furniture to make room for eight brand new bookcases we just bought to shelve the books we've hauled out of storage or re-purchased over the years. Yes, we both have Kindles, but there's nothing like sitting in a room lined with books and jumping up to grab an old favorite and thumb through it one more time.

# No Coot Like an Old Coot

George – July 12, 2004

I have never been a fan of public confession, but now I have to swallow my pride and proclaim my shortcomings. I have turned into an old coot. I never planned for it to happen. In fact, for years I have been in denial about it happening. But I can avoid the truth no longer.

There are things I believe for no reason at all. One earring in each ear is all anybody should wear. Tattoos may be fine for sailors, but for just about everybody else – especially girls – they are a sign of low intelligence. And people who don't eat animal flesh are all maladjusted neurotics and shouldn't be trusted around small children.

I can't justify these beliefs or defend them on any logical level. I believe them for one reason alone. I am an old coot. I like to wear my pants high and complain about the government. That's who I am.

Now that I've said it out loud, I must tell you something else. There's nothing wrong with being an old coot. In fact, it's a lot better than being a young fool. Young fools don't understand old coots, but old coots do understand young fools, because almost all old coots at one time in their lives were young fools. They know what makes young fools tick. They know why young fools make asses of themselves around women, why they want to challenge other young fools to fights in the parking lots of bars, and why they drive too fast, drink too much, and end up on lonely highways, howling at the moon.

Somewhere in the middle – between young fool and old coot – you find the responsible family man, punching a clock, earning a salary, and paying the bills.

Counting the days until he too can be an old coot.

# The Never-Changing Human

George – May 7, 2002

Most middle-aged and older people would like to be young again. Just ask them, and they'll tell you. But they always want to attach a condition to it, and it's always the same condition: It would be wonderful to be young again, but only if I knew then what I know now.

For instance, if we knew then, what we know now, we'd eat better, we wouldn't smoke or drink too much, and we'd work harder and not blow our money on stupid stuff. The problem is, if we did all those things, we wouldn't be young. We'd just be older people with good-looking skin, bodies that didn't ache, and half-a-century of life still ahead. And that's what most of us want – not youth. Just the obvious advantages of it.

It's kind of like after the oil boom went bust in Texas in the early 80s, and all the expensive homes were boarded up, the pools drained, and the sports cars repossessed. One of the common laments of the time was: Please Lord, let me do it again, and this time I won't spend it all on fast women and good-looking horses. We're sure there's a similar saying up in the Silicon Valley.

The truth is, if we were young again, most of us probably would do it all the same way again. Young people aren't dumb; they just have a different perspective. Life stretches out in front of them like an endless highway. They have no responsibilities. What's wrong with abusing your body if you can bounce back the next morning and feel as good as new?

If you felt now as good as you felt then, would you spend your time at work, putting in long hours, trying to get ahead? Or would you head for the beach to drink beer, lay in the sun, and ogle the opposite sex.

People may get old, but human nature remains the same.

# Killing Time

George and Carmela – March 17, 1997

We remember when we were young how time used to move, slow and easy like honey down the side of a biscuit. We were kids, and we spent a lot of our time just hanging out. Our whole lives were ahead of us, all our options were open, anything was possible. And if anybody asked what we were doing, we'd say we were "just killing time."

The problem is that the older we got, the faster time moved. When we were kids, minutes and hours and days dribbled away in slow motion. Now it's weeks and months and years shooting by so fast it takes our breath away. Life that took so long to get going, all of a sudden seems like a quick dash to the end.

Our theory is that when you're 5, one year is 20 percent of your life, and it feels like it. Three weeks to Christmas? It seemed like forever. But when you're 50, 20 percent of your life is ten years. Ten years now seems about the same as one year did back then.

We don't kill time anymore; we savor it. When time becomes available, we treat it with reverence and respect. And we wonder if this is how it ends, running full speed off the cliff like Thelma and Louise. Maybe not. Maybe when we get old, things will change. Maybe when the deadlines are past and a lifetime of appointments have been met, and our calendar books are empty, time will slow back down again. And we'll say: Hey Sweetie, let's get in the motorhome and head for Quartzite. Just to kill some time.

We should all live so long.

# Damn Kids!

George – November 13, 2016

We are pretty tough sometimes on the younger generation. We criticize them for being narcissistic, we lament their lack of work ethic, and we are stunned by their smug arrogance. The greatest generation was tested and toughened by depression and war. The new generation has been spoiled and weakened by affluence and entitlement.

But behind all our middle-age bluster and condemnation is a simple truth, a truth buried so deep that we either fail to recognize its existence or we are reluctant to recognize it for what it is. It is the same truth shared by every older generation that looks askance at the younger generations that follow.

We're jealous. We are jealous of how they wake up in the morning, full of vim and vigor. We are jealous of how they have a whole lifetime spread before them, full of possibilities and limited only by their imaginations. It's not that we want to deny young people the joys and benefits of youth.

What irritates us is that they don't seem to recognize or appreciate what they have. The whole world is spread out at their feet. All they have to do is reach out, choose a path, and start working toward their dreams. But they don't. They sit around, telling each other and anybody who will listen how bored they are, how unfair the world is, and how uptight adults are.

You're darn right we're uptight. We had our own time of unlimited possibilities, but it's over, and we miss it. That's because when we were their age, we were doing a lot of the same things that they are currently doing. But now we know better, and one of these days they will too. Unfortunately, when that day arrives, they'll probably be too old to do anything about it.

Except, of course, complain about the next generation.

# Putting Memories to the Music

George – May 14, 2001

OK, I admit it. I'm not part of the MTV generation. Jerky, out of focus, flickering images of sullen, pierced and tattooed young people, do nothing for me, which is another way of saying I'm over the age of 50 and I still have an attention span of more than three or four seconds.

In the olden days, we put our own personal images to music. You heard a song and it took you back to a time and place in your life. Certain songs reminded you of certain people, and each song meant different things to different folks.

Take the lyric. "I've got sunshine on a cloudy day, when it's cold outside, I've got the month of May."

Every time I hear the Temptations sing that line, it takes me back to 1965, sitting in the rain on a hilltop in the Central Highlands of Vietnam, thinking about home and worried about getting my butt shot off. It doesn't make sense. The song may bring up a totally different picture for most other people, but for me it will always be Vietnam.

Think what it would have been like if "My Girl" had been a video instead of just a song. There'd be a guy, then a girl, he'd be sitting at a window on a rainy day, she would show up, the sun would come out, the sun would go down, they'd have an argument, it would start to rain again, they'd get back together, the sun would come out.

In the old days, when you just heard the song, you had to use your imagination. You filled in the names and faces. Now you have somebody else to do it for you.

Somehow, it's just not the same.

31

# Sometimes it's Just TMI

George – June 8, 2009

The problem with growing older is there are some things you just don't get. You want to be the kind of person who gets things, and so you keep trying to "get it" and step-by-step, the rest of the world pulls you slowly into the future. Years ago I gave up on typewriters and started writing on a computer. Then I gave up writing letters and started sending emails. I gave up reading the newspaper and now turn to the internet to find out what is going on in the world.

Now, I've begun tweeting. I'm not entirely sure why I'm tweeting, but I hope it works out. If it doesn't, I am going to blame my friend Alexandra Spencer over at AECOM for talking me into tweeting. She said she thought it was crazy at first too, but has since changed her mind. She likes tweeting and convinced me that I will like it too.

In case you don't know about tweeting, it's what you do on Twitter. Twitter is a messaging site where people can send tweets to their friends or associates about what they are doing. And it's not just for kids. Movie stars are tweeting, politicians are tweeting, even high-powered executives are doing it. They're all atwitter over tweeting.

Here's how it works. The tweets must be brief because you only get 140 characters. Once you tweet, then all the people who have signed up to get your tweets know what you're up to. And if you want to know what they're up to, you follow them.

My nieces tweet, so I looked to see what they were tweeting. My niece Mallory said it was hot, she had a headache, and she was going to take some Tylenol. My niece Bailey said she had gone an entire week without eating meat and was feeling fine. My question is who cares?

When I have a headache, I also take Tylenol, and I have never in my life gone an entire week without eating meat, and I never intend to. However, I feel no compunction to tweet folks about it. Nonetheless, I've now begun tweeting with them both.

**EPILOGUE:** By 2020, the limit for tweet characters had been doubled, my nieces had fled to Instagram, and we had a President who would not stop tweeting. The great thing about it is that the U.S. president can communicate directly with every American. The bad thing about it is that the U.S. president can communicate directly with every American. Tweet. Tweet.

# A Do-Over Please

Carmela – October 5, 2019

At some time, you get to a point where you want a do-over in life. Not so you can be young and strong and beautiful again, but so that you can do everything better this time. So that you can do it right this time. So that you can say the right things, do the kind things, and choose to be quiet sometimes instead of talking all the time.

You get to the point where you understand that sometimes – often times – your opinion doesn't matter. You start to understand that just because you have a thought, that doesn't mean that the world needs to hear it. Even if it is a really, really good thought, it doesn't mean that you really, really must share it.

And that's the time when you start to want a do-over.

You want a do-over so you can give up the impatient tone and let go of the snotty remark – no matter how funny it is. It's a time when you realize that the conviction that you were absolutely, positively, surely right, might really have meant only that you were absolutely, positively, surely opinionated.

There is some peace in understanding that so many others are in the same boat.

As painful as regrets of words and deeds are, we are lucky to have them. When we have regrets is when, if we are very lucky, we get some glimmer of enlightenment – or maybe even redemption – even if we don't get the do-over.

# Adventures Along the Mortal Coil

George – October 7, 2017

I promise myself sometimes not to write so much about getting old. But you know it's just so funny, and there's just so much material, that I find it hard to resist.

Let's face it. Getting old is a hoot or at least it should be. And it goes without saying that growing old sure as Hell beats the alternative.

So I'm not complaining, even though this has been one of those months when everything seemed to fall apart. My wife and guardian angel is always nagging me to go see the doctor, which I hate. But then I have to remind myself that every day I enjoy now is because she pushed me to see a doctor at points in the past.

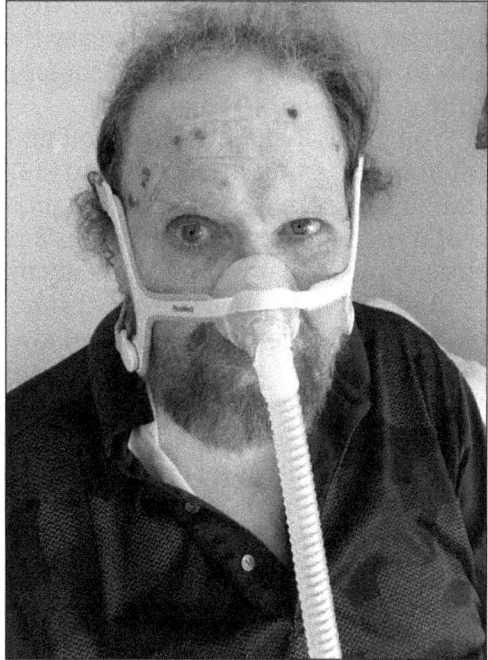

So, this month, I went to see the cardiologist, the dermatologist, the vascular surgeon, the sleep specialist, and a physical therapist.

The cardiologist gave me a clean bill of health – sort of – after a restless night hooked up to a monitor with sensors pasted to my body that left me with a rash.

The dermatologist sprayed me so vigorously with liquid nitrogen that I had open wounds along my arms and across my face. That will teach me not to go out without my sunscreen on.

The vascular surgeon recommended some knee-high pressure stockings for my varicose veins and a device for putting them on that can only be described oddly phallic.

The sleep specialist sent me home with an overnight monitor that showed my oxygen levels were too low and that I was failing to breathe several times an hour. He gave me a pressurized air mask to wear throughout the night, every night, probably for the rest of my life. We'll see about that.

I threw out my left knee and went hobbling around for a couple of weeks until it became so painful that I had to get a cane and a knee brace. My knee is getting better, but the doctor says I may still need a painful cortisone shot. My brother-in-law, who lives in Arizona and packs a gun everywhere he goes, warned me that he got such a shot in his knee and it hurt so much that he threatened to shoot the doctor if the doctor didn't pull out the needle and let him limp home.

My wife says I'm a sissy and that pain is part of life and that women understand that much better than men do, which just proves that not all sexists are male.

Despite the problems, I am feeling much better and happy as Hell to be on the other side of it – at least for now. Of course, there's still the possibility of the cortisone shot lurking someplace in the near future, but I'll cross that bridge when I come to it.

Despite what my wife may think, I am not a sissy. I'll even leave my gun at home.

# The Reluctant Healer

George – June 30, 2016

My wife Carmela would make a great nurse, even though she would hate it.

She hates hospitals, she hates all the messy blood and ooze, and most of all she hates sick people. Even with her own husband, after a couple of days, her patience wears thin. And then she starts asking, "are you going to get better now, or are you just going to keep lying around, moaning about how bad you feel?"

I will tell you this. The answer to that question is not sarcasm: Oh, I think I will lay around for a few more days, coughing and throwing up and moaning about how bad I feel. The correct answer is to stop feeling sorry for yourself, start moving your butt, and start feeling better.

The truth is that the tough-love school of nursing works. Pretty soon, you are feeling better, if for no other reason than you want to get strong enough to slap her dirty rotten face before you die. Of course, I exaggerate, but only a little.

When push comes to shove, Carmela rises to the occasion. She does what is required, whatever that is, however disgusting, nasty, and scary it may be. It's one of many reasons that I love her.

The latest such incident came right before we left for vacation. I went to my dermatologist for – among other things – a pre-cancer growth on the back of my left hand. The doctor sprayed the growth with liquid nitrogen, which is supposed to freeze it and cause it to fall off. Two days later, when we left for vacation, I had the mother-of-all boils on the back of my hand where the doctor had sprayed it.

It was ugly and gross, but I figured that just meant it was getting ready to fall off and leave behind a patch of pristine skin. So off we went, cutting across the desert in weather hot enough to make a scorpion eat his own tail.

But the mother-of-all blisters didn't go away. It just kept right on growing. By the time we pulled into Flagstaff, Arizona that night, it was bigger than ever, and by Gallup, New Mexico, the following day, it was beginning to ooze some nasty gunk. It was time for some hotel-room surgery. Carmela got some alcohol wipes from the First Aid kit she started carrying when I hit a certain age, sterilized a long thin needle and a pair of scissors, laid out a towel and began to operate. It was absolutely disgusting, but Carmela is very brave.

What Carmela has taught me in life is that you have to approach your problems straight on. You don't whine about it or complain, you just clench your jaw and do it.

Did it hurt? A little bit, but how could I feel sorry for myself, when Carmela was doing all the dirty work? The back of my hand is still scarred and ugly, but the big boil is gone and so is the pain.

What it comes to is this: In life, you do what you have to do, no matter how much you hate it.

Thank you for that insight, my dear.

# Incident in Checkout Lane Three

George – February 11, 2015

In my wife's family, there are code words for the kind of minor confrontation or embarrassment that occurs from time to time in everybody's life. In her family, such an occurrence is euphemistically referred to as "an incident," and it generally happens to a stubborn person – usually a woman – who has actually *caused* the incident.

An incident would include things like the time my wife harangued a mechanic who had charged us for a new radiator that cost several hundred dollars, when the real problem was a $12 thermostat.

"Are you a thief or an idiot," she yelled at the poor man.

"I am not a thief," he cried.

"Ah, she said, then you're an idiot."

In my wife's view, it had to be one or the other. There was no middle ground.

Or the time my mother-in-law got into a beef with a traffic cop who wrote her a ticket and insisted that she sign it. She refused, even though all she was signing was a promise to appear in court or pay the fine. He explained she had to sign it or he would have to take her to jail, something he really did not want to do to an 80-year-old woman. "Fine," she finally snapped. She grabbed the ticket from him and scrawled her name, adding at the bottom – "signed under duress."

I had an experience the other day at the supermarket. It was late. I was buying some milk, some chips, some bread, and some Velveeta. I was hungry, and I was in a hurry. There were only three people in line, my wife and me, and the man in front of us.

The cashier rang up his sale, and then asked him if he would like to contribute to some children's charity. What kind of charity, the man in front of me wanted to know, so the cashier explained. Then the cashier asked if the shopper wanted to have a special account that would provide him with discounts on specified items. The two talked about that for several minutes. Then there was the offer for a special discount on gasoline, in which participating customers got a discount from a certain gasoline company according to how many groceries they bought at the supermarket chain.

"Hmmm," the man said. "Let me call my wife." He had a short conversation with his wife, while I waited, hungry, tired, and

38

steaming in line.

The man in front of me finally reached an executive decision not to participate in the store's discount gasoline program – apparently on the advice of his wife, who I'm guessing was also waiting impatiently for him to finish his purchase and bring home the family food.

I finally reached the cashier with my groceries. How are you tonight, the clerk asked with a big friendly supermarket-approved smile on his face.

"Not so good, I tell him. I've been waiting in line a long time. How many transactions do you have to go through to sell somebody groceries?

"I'm just here to serve our customers," the clerk told me.

"I'm a customer too," I responded, "and I'm hungry and tired and waiting in line while you and "maybe-I-should-call-my-wife" boy discuss his next fill-up at the local gas station."

The clerk was no longer smiling. He was silently running my items across his little bar-code scanner, beep, beep, beep, and I'm thinking I'm almost out of here, when he asked me, "would you like to participate in our children's charity drive?"

I tensed up. After all I just said, the guy was now just screwing with me.

"I don't want to make a charitable contribution, I don't want to participate in any supermarket discount program, and I don't need any help buying gas from your affiliated gasoline chain since I can probably buy it cheaper at the station across the street. "All I want," I tell him, "is to give you some money, take my food, and go home."

No other words were exchanged. I paid for my items and received my change.

"My goodness," my wife said as I stalked from the store with my groceries.

"I think that qualifies as an incident." This coming from "Are-You-A-Thief-Or-An-Idiot" girl.

I take it as a compliment.

# Our friend Grant Young
# And the whole Young Family
### George and Carmela – August 23, 2020

Carmela and I don't agree with our friend, Grant Young on everything, but nobody ever asked us to – not Grant and not any of his family. In fact, a lot of his family don't always agree with him either, but that's OK. You don't have to agree to be a member of the extended Young family and friends.

It's an old-fashioned concept. People who see the world differently, getting along just fine with one another. As ex-officio members of the extended family, we end up being happy participants to a lot of holiday celebrations and get-togethers.

There's Grant's mother and father, Anne and Larry; his sister Elizabeth; his nephews Luke and Logan; and various unofficial members and family adoptees such as music teacher and composer Williametta Spencer; professor emeritus and music lover Maurice Meyerson; Elizabeth's friend Aliza; Grant's pal, gold prospector Dave Campbell; rancher and landholder Francine; the nephews' various girlfriends of the day, and of course Carmela and me.

But the nucleus for our membership in this not-so-elite group has been our friendship with Grant. There's a lot of things you can say about Grant. He is tough, sometimes prickly, opinionated, outspoken, generous, loyal, smart, and cynical.

What allows our friendship to be special is that it's OK to get angry, OK to argue, OK to laugh, and OK to complain about life. What makes Grant so special is that he is our fine and loyal pal and has been since he was in his 20s, Carmela was in her 30s and George was in his 40s.

Grant is not perfect. In fact, he can be a total curmudgeon. He gets cranky about things, and if you start to tell a funny story more than once, he is quick to tell you he has heard it before. His Midwestern roots go deep, and he'll have none of those shenanigans of embellishing what made the story funny the first time around.

What Grant never seems to realize is that for Italians like Carmela and Southerners like George, the stories get enhanced and funnier – if somewhat less accurate – as the years go by.

Everybody in the Young family and their adoptees accept the fact that Grant can be a little grumpy. His mother, on the other hand, is a total hoot – a musician and former teacher – who in her 80s is still riding bicycles on cross-country trips, traveling down rivers in canoes and camping out on the shore, shooting guns, and hitting the slopes each winter.

His dad is quieter, but equally as adventurous. The nephews eschewed college for work and adventure, and it was probably the best decision either of them ever made.

Everybody seems to accept that none of us is perfect, just as they accept the fact that Carmela waves her arms and hands around like she's conducting an orchestra when she expounds on any subject or that George sometimes tends to be quieter and moodier. Everybody in the group basks in the hospitality of the Young household.

It's always a hoot to go visit and even when it's not, it's still pretty damn good – a little sunshine in our lives, brought to us by our dear pal, Grant Young.

Something for which we are forever grateful.

# Blood Still Matters

George – November 6, 2020

Several years ago, I was reunited with my extended family – cousins from the bloodline of Ernest Lee Cunningham and Mertia Alice Hampton Cunningham, my grandparents from my father's side. It started, as do many such stories these days, on Facebook, when I received a message from my cousin Susan Cunningham Hencin, wondering if I was the long-lost cousin from the Cunningham side of the family.

I confessed that I was, although the last time I had seen Susan she was just a very little girl with skinny legs and a puffy dress.

Many decades earlier, when my mother and father split up, my mother went her own way and any further contact with my father and his family quickly dissolved. So I began to think of my family as my mother, my two brothers, and me. It was the four of us against the world and as the oldest son, it was my responsibility to step up and help make sure there was food on the table and a roof over our heads

It wasn't as though I was in charge. My mom called the shots, but I was her right-hand man and enforcer, keeping my younger brothers in line, making sure the work got done, and doing whatever it took to keep enough money coming in to support the four of us.

My kid brother Chuck died at 23 in a workplace accident, then years later my mom slipped away with a heart attack at 82, and finally my tough and lovely little brother Bill passed, leaving me the sole survivor of my small clan.

I got the query on Facebook sometime not long before Bill died.

Was I the same George Cunningham who grew up in Florida and had cousins named Susan, Linda, Gary, Nancy, Mike, and Steven? That was me, I replied. And suddenly I was reconnected.

There was a reunion of sorts in which I frankly was a less-than-enthusiastic participant. The last time I had seen these folks, the boys were in short pants and most of the girls had frilly little petticoats. Gary, the only son of my Uncle Jim, had died of a heart attack before we linked up. The rest of my long-lost cousins were now senior citizens.

I told myself that these people meant little to me. I hadn't seen or thought about them in years. But Carmela is of Italian heritage as they say, and family ties are important. She convinced me to reconnect.

As it turned out, all the children of Ernest and Myrtle were dead except for one, my Uncle Calvin Charles Cunningham, a fragile old man who lived in Raleigh, North Carolina. We corresponded, and he sent some pictures he had of my mother as a young child, for which I am forever grateful, and we made plans to get together the next time Carmela and I were back East.

But Uncle Cal died before that happened, which in a strange twist made me the patriarch of the clan – the oldest member of the surviving generations of Cunninghams. During those first years, my cousins and I started crafting a new relationship for our old family. It wasn't like we picked up where we had left off – with a bunch of us cousins leaning against Granddad Cunningham's car – all lined up between our grandparents. The reality was a bunch of stilted phone calls and meetings and emails.

It wasn't just the passage of time that separated my Cunningham Cousins and me. It also was the life experience and attitudes. The daughters of my Uncle Jim worked in education and one of my Uncle Hank's sons is a college professor. My attitude toward teachers is less than positive. I love knowledge, but I have always hated school. It was true when I was a kid, and it is still true today. Uncle Hank's other son is an engineer and musician – a lovely combination and one to which I can easily relate.

What do we have in common? Mostly just blood. But as my wife already knew and I was to discover, blood matters. Politics is just politics, religion is just different views of whatever big truth to which you subscribe, but family is family.

And, in the end, they are all my family. Do I have my favorites? Of course. But as Carmela says, they are all entitled to one of my kidneys if they need it.

That's an easy promise to make. Most of my organs these days are all used and abused from 80 years of hard living. So, what's left to offer?

My share of the legacy of Ernest Lee and Mertia Alice – long dead, but not forgotten – whose genes we all share, and whose attitudes and love live on, however diluted, in each and every one of us.

# When Family Comes Late to the Game

Carmela – November 11, 2020

I come from a big Italian family. I have lots of brothers and sisters, nieces and nephews, uncles, aunts and cousins. The most fun are often the cousins. They're close enough to love and fight with, but not quite so close as siblings who you have to battle for parent's time, control of the TV, whose turn it is to do the dishes, and your own unique identity. I was in my late 50s when I learned that there was something *even better* than cousins.

Cousins-in-law.

I was disappointed when early on George told me that he had lost all contact with his cousins so long ago that the girls "wore Mary Janes and frilly dresses that stuck out this far." He had some stories about them, but nothing I could really sink my teeth into.

"Don't you want to look them up," I'd ask. And he'd reply, "they're senior citizens now. I don't even know if they're alive."

He was half-right. Like us, they are senior citizens. But most of his cousins are still alive. And as it turned out, they found us.

One day, these delightful Southern women tracked us down on Facebook and started emailing us. Before we even had the chance to visit them, Cousin Nancy pulled our photos off Facebook and included them in a Cunningham Family Calendar. When we did visit Nancy, her husband Roger, her sister Susan and husband Jim, sister Linda and husband Byron, and Cousin Mike, it went nicely. There were enough stories of them all being kids and going to the same schools together to keep the conversation going. But not a lot more.

What struck me that first day though, was how these strangers would call George "Corky" and his brother Chuck "C.K." and his brother Willie, "Billy." These new cousins actually knew those little boys – and loved them. They knew about them – and they talked about them like I talk about my own blood cousins.

George wasn't sure we'd go back after that first visit, but he hadn't grown up with the force that is Nancy. If Nancy decides she's pulling the family together – as she often does – then she's pulling the family together. And nothing "Corky" says is going to change that.

We took to visiting these new cousins every time we were in Florida, and I found out something really neat. Sometimes you just click with people. George, Henry the Wonder Dog, and I started spending more time with Nancy and Roger – in person, through email, texting, and on the phone. They love Henry, and every year when we go back to Florida, as soon as we turn into their neighborhood, Henry starts getting antsy in the car, and when his Aunt Nancy and Uncle Roger open their front door to greet us, Henry jumps out of my arms runs up the porch, past them and into the house, where there are always toys and treats and fresh water waiting for him.

Roger is an artist and Nancy writes children's books. Early on, Roger dubbed us the "Fabulous Four," and we have had great times working on each other's books, encouraging each other, wandering around Gulfport, talking into the night, and sitting around their house with Cousin Mike playing his guitar and us singing old Beach Boys tunes. Nancy passes around cymbals and mariachis and when there aren't enough to go around, she'll play the spoons. Roger joins on the harmonica. We are so bad, my sides almost split from laughing so hard. One night we got Roger to do a dance of seven veils while we played our goofy instruments and sang off key. We weren't even drunk.

Roger crafts life-size humans and animals out of styrafoam, plaster and paint. The first time I was in Roger and Nancy's home, I fell in love with a four-and-a-half-foot tall blue heron he had made. Two visits later, as he and I lounged on the couch shoulder-to-shoulder, hands clasped over our bellies, feet up on the coffee table, looking at the heron, Roger said in his slow, quiet drawl, "I think it's time."

"For what," I asked.

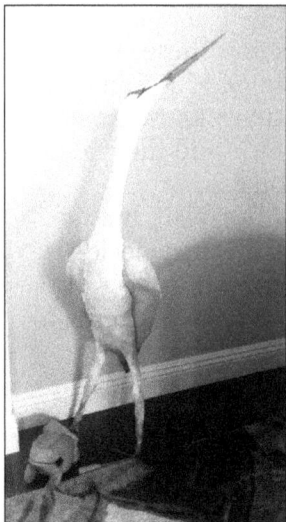

"For the bird to go home with you."

I named him Horatio Hunter, and he stands guard in our living room. He's since been joined with a three-foot long tortoise named Hadrian, and Esmeralda, a bare-breasted old mermaid that Roger carved out of wood.

We have fun with Nancy and Roger, and we love Nancy and Roger. If I don't get a text or email from them every day or so, I get kind of worried.

Because that's how it works with family – no matter how long it takes you to find them.

# Taking Retirement a Step at a Time
## Carmela – August 26, 2002

A friend started talking about retiring in two years – at 50 – and I was jealous. I still see stretching ahead, years of getting up early and working late, with only a few weeks a year to lounge around and call my own. Even then, I have a laptop and email connection to make sure I stay in touch with the demands back at the office.

I started longing for retirement too, but then it hit me. If I did retire at 50, and if I was lucky enough to reach old age, I'd have 30 or more years with no demands, no traffic, and no particular place to be.

There are people who have productive, happy retirements. They're the ones with the part-time jobs, and the ones at the community center teaching kids to read. They're planning concerts, driving up the coast with their mates, and reading all those plaques that are posted at historical sites. They see every single National Park, and they go to every one of the 50 states. Then they start in on Europe and South America. They're doing the things we long to do as we sit on the 710 Freeway, wishing the trucks would move a little faster.

Time is always moving at the wrong speed – racing ahead while we try to cram in time with mates and kids and friends and interesting jobs, and then slowing far too much when we have little to do. Kids – out of school for the summer – complain that they're bored, while more than one long-retired friend has longed for the days of rushing around to get everything done.

The answer, of course, is simple. Don't stop working when you're 60, just work a little less when you're 40. Don't wait until you're 70 to garden, start digging your fingers and toes in the dirt when you're 30. Don't wait until you're 80 to travel, take a trip this week.

Time will never be on our side. All we can do is outfox it for a while.

# Chapter 2: Those we Loved ... and Lost

**Preface:** There's this thing we started doing when we got into our later middle years. We started saying "I love you" more. Not to each other or family, we always did that. We started saying it to long-time friends. We'd have long, four-way chats on the phone and end with "love you guys." We'd see friends for lunch or dinner, and we'd hug Hello and Good-bye, and mumble "love you" as we walked away. It wasn't too hard for me, but for George, it was a bit of a challenge for those mumbles to get clearer and bolder. The hugging other guys part was kind of a challenge for him too. It started like he and his pals were joking – making fun of the "twig boys" who'd hug each other all the time. But at some point, more emotion got packed in. It's a good thing too. One day, he hugged a long-time friend we'd just had lunch with, mumbled something close to "love you guy..." and drove away. It was the last time we ever saw our friend. Two days later, he was dead.

*Carmela*

# Essays

| | |
|---|---|
| Let Me Feed the Daisies | 52 |
| Old Age and Corny Jokes | 53 |
| My Kind and Imperfect Grandfather | 54 |
| My Father, Myself | 58 |
| My Mother's Big Secret | 67 |
| The Tough Old Woman I Adored | 70 |
| My Boy's Mother | 73 |
| The End of the Line | 74 |
| Charles 'Chuck' Cunningham, Better Known as 'C.K.' | 77 |
| The Softest Tough Guy I Ever Knew | 84 |
| My Brother Bill, Who Broke My Heart | 88 |
| My High-Flying Uncle Hank | 90 |
| The Day the Children Would Not Stop Crying | 94 |
| Silent Joe | 97 |
| First Love and a Twice Broken Heart | 100 |
| My Pal: Larry LaRue 1949-2017 | 102 |
| The Last Time I Saw Betsy | 108 |
| Tombstone Territory | 111 |

# Let Me Feed the Daisies

## George - September 15, 2005

Something happened to me the other day that hasn't happened in years. I was scrambling some eggs for breakfast, when I cracked open the last one, and it was fertile. Back in the old days, when I found blood in an egg, I was irked. After all, eggs cost money.

Instead, I found myself vaguely cheered by the discovery. Somewhere, somehow, a crafty rooster had gotten through security at the egg factory and made a little whoopee with his hen friend. No matter how much we try to civilize and sanitize the world, life always seems to triumph.

Have you ever stood on an expanse of asphalt that goes on and on, acre after acre, and right in the middle you find a dandelion growing in a crack, little yellow petals towering over the petrochemical tar? It's life forcing its way past every obstacle, saying "I'm here world and I'm not going away."

A giant asteroid may have killed the dinosaurs. And, who knows, we may yet blow ourselves to smithereens before we're through. But life, in some form or another, will continue. You see it in a blood-stained yolk and in the tiny dandelion waving in the breeze. It will not be denied.

Even in death, life goes on. They are many colorful ways to say somebody died. He gave up the ghost, he kicked the bucket, he bought the farm. But my favorite is, he's pushing up daisies. That's what I want to do – push up daisies. I don't want to be stuck away in some hermetically sealed casket, pickled and preserved. I want to lie there naked when the spring rains turn the ground into slush and the little daisy sprouts send their roots down to feed on my corpse.

I'll go meet my maker – after I'm through fertilizing the flowers.

# Old Age and Corny Jokes

George – January 21, 2008

I notice as I get older that my jokes get cornier. As a younger man, I might have worried about this, but as an old coot it doesn't bother me. I seem able to observe my humor from afar, almost as a neutral observer, watching myself tell some stupid story and thinking as I tell it, isn't this interesting? Does George really think that's funny?

Maybe it's because when I grew up I hung out at lot with my grandfather, and the older I get, the more like him I become. He always told corny jokes, and as a little kid, I thought he was the funniest person I had ever met.

For instance, my grandfather drove everywhere at 25 miles-an-hour or less. If we were going 100 miles, it took at least four hours to get there. And everybody in the family would tease him about it.

One day he said to them, "you laugh, but the other day I passed a car that was doing 50." Then he paused for a moment – my grandfather had great timing – and added: "Of course, it was going in the other direction."

And nobody laughed harder than me. I thought my grandfather was right up there with Jack Benny and Bob Hope.

Another time, I was driving with my grandfather and we passed a graveyard. And he said, very seriously, "you know they won't bury us in that cemetery."

I asked, "why not?" I was a wonderful straight man, which may have been why we got along so well. And he said, "because we're not dead," and I laughed so hard my sides hurt, and it became our joke. Every time we passed a cemetery from then on, I would ask him, "will they bury us there," and he'd look real serious and shake his head no, and I'd ask him why. And then he'd tell me, and we'd laugh just like neither of us had heard it before.

But this is not about my grandfather, it's about me and my sense of humor. My grandfather has been dead for many, many years, but I sometimes wonder if he ever checks in on me.

And I wonder if I can still make him laugh.

# My Kind and Imperfect Grandfather
## George – August 23, 2020

My kind and imperfect grandfather taught me about life. Grandparents and grandchildren have a kind of connection that parents and children never get.

I had that kind of connection with my grandfather. I was the first-born grandchild of Ernest Lee Cunningham and his wife, Mertia Alice Hampton Cunningham and they both spoiled me, but especially my grandfather, because unlike my mother or my grandmother, my grandfather understood little boys.

And, he knew how to spoil them. My mother and I lived with my grandparents during World War II, and I adored the old man.

Like a lot of little boys in that era, I loved trains. My grandfather knew when the train left the station in downtown St. Petersburg, and he knew about how long it took to cross 37th Street, about a mile north of where we lived on Queensboro Avenue. Every evening, we would walk down to Queensboro Avenue and 37th Street and stand there waiting for the train to cross the road, and every evening when the train came through the intersection, blowing it's horn, we would wave – the old man and me – at the train passing through.

Then we would walk back home.

We were pals, the old man and me.

One time, he took me to the stop where the train picked up passengers in downtown St. Petersburg, and I got to go up in the locomotive, meet the engineer, and sit in his seat. It was a glorious experience, which I still remember more than 70 years later.

The old man also indulged me in ways of which my mother and

my grandmother did not approve. One thing we would do when I was out with him was go to eat at a cafeteria, where I could order anything I wanted as I went down the line. My typical order would be mashed potatoes, gravy and biscuits, cake, ice cream, pie, custard, and Jell-O.

Neither my mother nor my grandmother were amused, but it didn't seem to bother my grandfather at all. Like many men of his time, winning the approval of women was not high on his list of priorities.

He sometimes drank to excess. He flirted with pretty girls. He chewed tobacco, spitting the juice into an empty Maxwell House coffee can when need be. And he had a wonderful sense of humor.

In many ways he was like a little boy himself.

When my father returned from the war, we moved not very many blocks away and on Saturday night, the family would visit at my grandfather's and grandmother's apartment over the garage behind my Uncle Hank's house. These were special times for kids to listen and learn about life.

One of the things I used to do, if the grown-up conversation turned to people I didn't know or stories I had already heard, was go into the bathroom where my grandfather kept his shaving mug – a cup with a cake of shaving soap in it – a shaving brush, and his double-edged safety razor. Back in the day, the double-edged blade was inserted into the safety razor holder and removed when you were done with it.

My game was to lather up my grandfather's shaving brush, apply the suds to my 8-year-old face, then shave it off with the razor holder, which was safe since it had no blade in it. I would twist my face, applying short little strokes beneath my nose and bottom lip as I had seen my grandfather and father do, finish up, wipe the remaining suds off my face and examine how good I looked in the mirror.

Except one night, my grandfather had left the blade in the razor and as I did my little razor game, I noticed that blood was trickling out from all the little nicks and cuts I had made during my shaving pantomime. I was in a panic. Not because of the blood. I was an active kid, so I was used to bruises and blood.

No. It was because my little shaving game would be exposed and I would look foolish in the eyes of all the grownups. I tore off some toilet paper, dabbed at all the bloody places until they stopped bleeding, flushed the bloody paper down the toilet, and went back into the living room with nobody the wiser.

And it worked, as long as I kept a perfectly straight face. But as soon as I began to talk or answer questions, the cuts opened up again and soon there were trickles of blood running down my face.

My mother was in a panic.

"What happened," she demanded. And I gave the same answer that little boys always give in such circumstances.

"Nothing."

Obviously, the jig was up and I finally had to confess, much to the amusement of all the grownups, and to my great shame.

My grandfather – who had to be totally amused – took it in good spirits. He never teased me too much. In my family, you had to be tough. Part of the job is getting teased. If you wanted to be part of the family, you had to be able to take a little ribbing.

As I got a little bit older, things got more serious in our town. We lived in a poor white section, not far from the poor black session. But things were changing. Black people were beginning to buy property outside their area. Nobody called it the ghetto back them. They called it N****r Town.

My uncles were outraged. The South would rise again, they vowed. The next thing you knew black people would be wanting to go to school with white children. The situation was both dire and scary for a kid.

I went to my expert in such matters – my grandfather.

What is going to happen? I asked. Nothing, he said. Black people aren't very different from white people. They will move into white neighborhoods and everybody will learn to get along.

Was he really that naïve? I don't think so. I think it was an answer suitable for a young boy, getting ready to enter the treacherous realm of puberty, and probably it was part wishful thinking. My grandfather was a hopeful man but also a man of his times.

Nowhere was that more sadly apparent than in his relationship with Woodrow – his helper at the ice company where he worked. My grandfather was a handyman – a carpenter, a plumber, and mechanic – whatever was needed.

His helper was a black person named Woodrow. I don't know Woodrow's last name, but he and my grandfather became very close. They were more than workmates. They were friends. But they both lived in the world as it was.

56

Woodrow never came to my grandfather's house for dinner, and my grandfather never went to Woodrow's home. They were close, but their friendship was limited to working side-by-side.

My grandfather died of a heart attack in 1958, climbing the stairs to his apartment over the garage. He was 66 years old.

Woodrow was there at my grandfather's funeral, sitting alone at the back of the church. He left when it was over, and I never heard of or saw him again.

But when I think of my grandfather, I don't think of a man caught in a time and place in which he had to conform to an acceptable code of behavior whether he believed in it or not.

I think of a man who enjoyed life with all its limitations and restrictions – a man who made a decision to live his life, rather than spend his days railing against the unfairness of it.

In other words, a man not that unlike myself.

# My Father, Myself

George – October 24, 2019

I spent many years of my life hating my father, scorning him, and harboring bitter feelings about him long after he was dead and buried.

Ernest Lee Cunningham Jr. fell short when it came to being a man, being a provider, being a father, and staying sober for more than a few days at a time. He was a failure and a spendthrift, and I despised him for it.

I was 13 when my father walked out of our ramshackle home – a square, unpainted, concrete-block house with an uncovered concrete floor and interior walls smeared with tar and painted over with silver paint. My grandfather had slathered the tar on the interior of the outside walls, apparently when he was drunk and under the impression that the tar would help insulate the place. The silver paint was added later, I suppose because it was the only free paint available at the time.

We had no water heater or kitchen stove. My mother cooked on a two-burner electric hot plate. For baths, she would get a big pot of water, put it on the hot plate until the water was boiling, then pour it into the bathtub and add cold water until the bath water was about two inches deep and lukewarm.

That seemed fine with my father.

I inadvertently came upon a picture of my childhood home a couple of years ago when I was looking through some snapshots gathered by members of my extended family. The sight of it was gut-wrenching. I quickly closed the box of photos and put them down even though I had only looked through about half of the pictures.

My first memory of my father was when I was almost 5 years old. I was born in 1940, one year, one week, and two days before the Japanese bombed Pearl Harbor. My father soon after joined the Army, went overseas, and didn't come back into my life until 1945, after the end of the war. My two younger brothers were born in 1946 and 1948.

Some years later, when my father left for places unknown, I became the man of the house. My mother and I got up every day at 3 a.m., got 700 newspapers, stuffed them with inside sections, put rubber bands on them in dry weather, put them in waxed bags when it was raining, and drove our car through dark roads delivering to subscribers. We did this seven days a week, 365 days a year. On weekends and evenings, I would collect for the paper from the customers, mow lawns, and pick up other odd jobs washing dishes or doing gardening work. We didn't go on vacation or holiday. The money I earned went to support the family.

I was tired all the time, and each day when the alarm went off at 3 a.m., I hated my father a little more.

In 1965, I was serving with the 173rd Airborne Infantry in Okinawa when my company commander called me to his office and told me my father was dying. My brother Charles Kenneth Cunningham – C.K. to the family – was stationed on the DMZ in Korea at the time. We both got 30-day leaves to return to the states.

I visited my father one time at the Bay Pines VA Hospital in Florida during those 30 days, and I stayed for about 30 minutes.

We had nothing to talk about.

While I was on leave, my unit shipped out from Okinawa to Vietnam. My brother ended up stationed with a Special Forces unit in the Mekong Delta.

My father didn't die during my leave. I finally learned that he was dead when I caught up with my unit at a base camp near Vung Tau on the southern coast of Vietnam. I shrugged the news off. I had signed up to be in a war – to join that elite group of patriots who represent their country on the battlefield – and here I was.

It was near Vung Tau that I experienced my first combat. A sniper fired a couple of shots at us from a tree line. He was less a sniper than some pissed-off Viet Cong local who decided to welcome us to the party and then split before we opened up on him.

We stood there stunned at the reality that somebody was

59

actually trying to kill us, until one of the Non-Coms, who had served in a war zone yelled for everybody to get down. We finally ended up at a base camp outside the airport at Bien Hoa, and spent the next year flying around the country in helicopters and C-130s – D-Zone, the Central Highlands, the Iron Triangle, the Plain of Reeds – dropping in on the enemy, killing some of them, being killed by some of them, and raising all kinds of general Hell.

My father was dead and buried, but I didn't forget or forgive him. I hated his memory with a passion.

I remember when I was in my 50s, my mother was talking about my father, not in an unkind way, and it frustrated me.

How can you be so forgiving, I wanted to know. He left us, walked out the door, and never looked back. We had no money. We ate chicken gizzards and hamburger mixed with white bread in order to make a pound of meat feed a woman and three hungry young boys.

My mother looked at me with a sad smile.

"He didn't walk out on us," she said. "I told him to go away and not come back. It was my choice, not his. He didn't want to go."

My mom was tough. She was not going to put up with my father spending his nights in bars, coming home late, smelling of perfume and booze. It was time for him to go.

Your father was a weak man, she told me. But she loved him dearly.

Still, I could not rid myself of the anger I had harbored for so long. My father could have sent her child support. He could have checked in to make sure we were OK. But he did not.

I have now lived 30 years longer than my father did. And I have grown more tolerant as I've gotten older and dealt with my own shortcomings.

I look back now from the perspective of age and I think one of the reasons I hated him so much, was that in many ways, I am like him. Easily diverted from whatever I am doing to anything new that catches my eye. Undisciplined. Willing to spend hours daydreaming about things that are never going to happen. Not particularly interested in making a lot of money or owning a lot of stuff.

And I fight it, the way all adult children fight the attitudes that they disliked in their parents but recognize in themselves.

Now I am old enough to realize that the hatred I felt for my father was a weight I carried on my shoulders for most of my adult life. Last year I made a deliberate decision to put down that burden and see my father for what he was – a sad and beaten man, ashamed of the life he had led, and ready to die.

My father was long dead. So was my mother. It was time to let it go.

And so I did.

It was not as hard as I thought.

Forgiving my father and freeing myself had unexpected benefits. Once I got past my hatred, I was able to recall and appreciate some of the better memories I had of him before my mother told him to hit the road.

I was one year old when my father left to go to war. I was five when he returned. During the war, my mother and I lived with my grandparents on the south side of St. Petersburg, Florida. My first memory of my father was when I woke up one morning and found him in bed with my mom. I'm sure he was happy to see me. I was probably not that sure about meeting him.

My father was a complex man – gregarious, combative, funny, angry, loving, hateful, weak, and strong. In other words, a person not that unlike me.

My father was a hard worker with a direct approach to finding a job. During the depression, he would go downtown, start on one side of the street and stop in every shop, store, and restaurant to ask for a work. If they didn't have an opening, he would offer to work for free in order to prove himself. He could be charming, funny, and persuasive. And by the end of the day, he usually had a job and a little bit of cash to take home.

Because of his kinky hair, my father's nickname and the name he most often went by was "Kink." I inherited my curly hair from him, hair that when it grew out would form little cork-screw ringlets. My nickname was "Corky."

I remember the early days of my parents' marriage as both happy and loving. I recall being allowed to go with my mother and father and my Uncle Hank and his wife May to a little diner,

61

owned by Johnny, an Army buddy of my father. The grownups would be smoking and telling stories of their dreams and adventures, and I would sit silently – children did not interrupt in those days – soaking it all in.

After a long dinner, the grownups would snub out their cigarettes onto their plates, and we would all go home, me a little wiser to the ways of the world than when we had arrived. It was a good time for my father and mother, and their love for one another was apparent.

I also learned about life in those early days, when my father, my Uncle Hank, and I would go gigging at night on the shallow-water flats of Boca Ciega Bay, a Coleman white-gas lantern mounted on the bow of a rented skiff. One person would stand at the bow, the gig held aloft, ready for action.

Fish, attracted to the light, would suddenly appear and the gig would fly – aimed high to compensate for the refraction of light through the water. The speared fish would be retrieved on the end of the gig and laid in the boat to be dismembered, cleaned, and its flanks cut into filets to be taken home for dinner.

One night a large fish suddenly appeared at the bow and the gig flew and connected. But this time, it wasn't the usual prey. It was a small shark that came out of the water mortally wounded, but fighting mad.

It was immediately eviscerated, decapitated, and cut into pieces. This was not a time when people commonly ate shark, so my father and my uncle hatched a plan to fool my mother and my aunt. And since I was a witness, I was included in the plot, which made me one of the guys playing a trick on the girls.

The plan was that we were going to tell the women that we had gigged an exotic fish called a "caribou." A caribou, of course, is another name for a reindeer, but we lived in Florida and neither my mother nor my aunt had ever heard of a caribou.

And it worked. My mother and my aunt raved about the caribou, which had none of the pesky little bones that sometimes made eating other fish a pain in the neck. And then when my father and my uncle finally told their wives that it was actually a shark, the women-folk were amazed.

I always remember it as a time that my dad and my uncle and I fooled the women. And I found out that I like teasing women, even if they were my mother and my aunt.

Then there was the time that I went on my first date at about 12 years old with a girl whose name I can't even remember. I had on a sports coat that had been handed down from one of my uncles, and which extended past my knuckles by more than an inch.

We rode along in silence for a little bit, my father driving and my date sitting between us in the front seat. And then my dad pulled out a pack of Camels, shook a couple of smokes part way out, and offered one to my date.

"No thank you, Mr. Cunningham," she said in a quivering little voice.

My father, who had started smoking at about age nine or 10, thought I was positively backward for being 12 and still not sucking down the smokes. He shrugged it off, lit one for himself, and drove us to the school.

Maybe the proudest I ever was of my father, however, was the time when I got out of the bath and he noticed a huge black-and-blue bruise across both my butt cheeks. I confessed that I had been punished for mouthing off to a teacher – another way I was like my father – and been sent to the Dean of Boys, a guy named Richard Jones, for punishment.

Back in the day, corporal punishment was allowed at school and Dean Jones had a huge paddle, he cleverly called the "board of education." He told me to bend over and grab the edge of his desk, then he swung like a batter swinging at a fast ball, and it hit me square across my butt and it hurt like Hell.

I hadn't mentioned it to my father because I thought I would be in trouble all over again. But I wasn't.

In fact, my father stormed down to the school, went into the Dean's office, and challenged him then and there to a fist fight. You want to hit somebody, he told him, then here I am, let's step outside and settle this now.

You have a problem with my son, you tell me and I will handle the punishment.

Dean Jones, the sniveling little shit that he was, backed down.

I wasn't sure at the time whether my father was defending me or was just in a jurisdictional dispute over who got to hit me. It was probably a little of both. But I have to say that I can't recall my father ever hitting me, either before or after the incident with Jones.

But as time went on, my father's wandering ways and inability to keep a job began to weigh on my parents' marriage. He would have a job for a few weeks, then get restless or angry over some

imagined or real slight and be ready to move on. And each time it happened, there was a financial toll that it took.

Among his jobs was driving a tanker-truck for Gulf Oil. He then talked his way up to being a company TBA salesman (Tires, Batteries and Accessories) for Gulf service station franchisees. After that he worked selling aluminum siding, and as a door-to-door salesmen selling leather-bound bibles to poor Southerners, who couldn't afford them.

He would start his own businesses, and each time he launched a new venture, he would print up a few hundred business cards. He was the "Shade-Tree Mechanic," who would come to wherever your car was broken down and work on it there. He had a meat-block cutting business with a machine that shaved off the top of a butcher's chopping block to smooth out the cuts and dents. He started a landscaping business in which I supplied the labor, and he made the deals and kept the money.

One scheme that got him into trouble was a wholesale egg business in which he convinced a chicken farmer down in Sarasota County to sell him eggs wholesale and let him pay with a post-dated check. The idea was that by the time the date on the check was reached, my father would have sold the eggs at a profit to restaurants or hotel dining establishments and deposited the money in his account.

My father was a great salesman, but unfortunately, not so great a businessman.

For one thing, he ran a cash business, and he loved running around with a big wad of bills held together by a money clip. He was drinking throughout the day by then – his beverage of choice being "blackberry brandy," which was not really like drinking real liquor. When he went to a local tavern for some real drinks, he would peel off a few bills and buy drinks for his bar buddies. He liked being the big spender.

What he didn't like was keeping books. It was not really his way to be writing down all his transactions in a ledger someplace. My father's thing was making deals. Writing it down somewhere was mundane and boring.

The big egg business problem was that he rented a unit in a cold storage warehouse to keep the eggs cool while they were waiting to be sold. Unfortunately, the egg unit happened to be situated next to a unit in which onions were being stored. The eggs absorbed the onion flavor through their shells – bringing harsh criticism from my father's customers.

The other problem was that the postdated check bounced, then bounced again, and again. The farmer filed a criminal complaint against my father, who had to explain to my mother what had gone wrong.

One might ask how I know all these details, since I was just a child at the time. The answer is, I don't.

I wasn't there when my father made the deal with the farmer or when he bought drinks for his friends at the bar, or when he had to destroy onion-contaminated eggs. But I was a precocious boy, who listened a lot to adult conversations and disputes, and could I reconstruct my version of the facts behind the words.

Although I grew up in Florida, my father's family came from the mountain country of Tennessee and Kentucky. And my father had inherited a bit of the Tennessee conman ethic.

Like the car polish he sold at county fairs. He would get an onlooker with an old beat-up automobile to volunteer the car for a demonstration. Then he would find the most tarnished and faded spot on the hood and polish it up. The results were amazing. The spot on the hood looked almost brand new. Then he would sit back and collect money from all the rubes – including the owner of the old car he used for the demonstration.

The only problem with the car polish was that it stripped off the top coat of paint on the car. Once you used it three or four times, you were down to bare metal.

Then there was the "EAT" sign that he sold to road-side restaurants all over the South. It was a bright sign shaped like an arrowhead with the word "EAT" in the middle, surrounded by a string of light bulbs. Once the sign was turned on, it flashed EAT, EAT, EAT over and over again.

My father had a traveling setup in which he would plug in the sign and demonstrate its hypnotic power. The sign, he promised, would increase the restaurant's business by 20 to 30 percent. All they had to do was put down half of the sign's cost and pay the other half when it was delivered from the home office.

The rub, of course, was that there was no home office, there was only one sign, and my dad had it. He pocketed the money and went on his way in search of a new sucker.

As I get older, I am convinced that my mother and my father loved one another. But contrary to what you might read in romance books or see in the movies, love does not conquer all.

So my father left. And when he did come back it was to check into the Veterans Administration Hospital at Bay Pines where he was diagnosed with terminal cancer. Perhaps because he was ashamed of his life and how he had let his family down, he did not contact his wife or sons. He only told my Uncle Henry that he had cancer and was dying and asked him not to tell anybody else.

But word leaked out, and I came back from Okinawa and my brother from Korea. It must have been distressing for him to see

how uncomfortable we all were with him - my younger brothers
too young to remember him clearly, and me too bitter to
acknowledge any affection or love I might have had.

I would change that if I could. But death makes such
sentiments meaningless. You can't undo the past.

If I could, I would.

# My Mother's Big Secret

## George – October 27, 2019

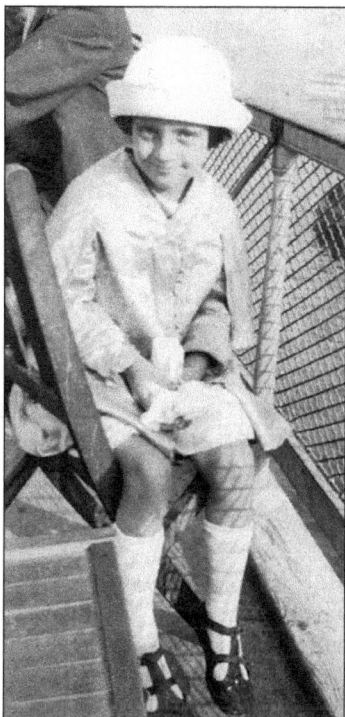

My mother, born Florence Georgine Davis, was raised by her father as an only child without a mother, brothers, sisters, cousins, aunts, uncles or grandparents. She grew up in a world without babies or older women to teach her by example about mothering a child or about being part of an extended family.

It marked her life, my life and the lives of my two younger brothers.

The story that I grew up with was that my grandmother died in childbirth and my grandfather and my mother moved from New York City to St. Petersburg, Florida when she was about 8 or 9. That turned out to be a big lie.

The truth turned out to be much more complex, as I was to find out later in life.

We need to talk, my mother told me. I was in my 50s; my mother in her 70s. The "we-need-to-talk" message chilled me to the bone. My imagination immediately when to the worst possible scenario. Cancer, death, or some other debilitating disease.

But here's the story I got – a story she never shared with my father or my brother Chuck, who was killed in a construction accident many years before.

My maternal grandmother did not die in childbirth as I had believed for my entire life.

My grandmother placed my mother in a boarding house at an early age, then went on about her life. When my grandfather – her estranged husband – wanted to visit his daughter, my grandmother would demand money or other gratuities from him.

My mother hated living in the boarding house and loved it when my grandfather would arrive and take her out, but it was always for too short a period and then she had to return to her lonely life.

My grandfather – fed up with how his daughter was being raised – finally "kidnapped" my mother when she was 8 or 9 years old. They boarded a train, and he took her from New York City where she was born to St. Petersburg, Florida, where he gave her the cover story about her mother's death.

She never saw her mother again.

That may sound like a big deal, but it wasn't the bombshell news that my mother needed to tell me. The big bombshell news was that my grandmother was Jewish. And since Jewish heritage is a maternal affair, handed down from mother to child it meant my mother was Jewish and so were my brothers and me.

Then as now, there was still a strain of anti-Semitism that ran through the nation and was especially strong in the Bible-Belt South. The Jews, after all, were the ones supposedly responsible for the crucifixion of Christ.

St. Petersburg was a tourist town that depended on snowbird visitors from the north to maintain its economy. And like all tourist towns, St. Pete loved the money that tourists brought, but hated the tourists themselves.

One of the jokes making the rounds at the time was: Happiness is a New York Jew going home with a Canadian under each arm.

The stereotype was that Jews were pushy, arrogant, and demanding. My mother, who was raised by her father, kept her Jewish heritage to herself her entire life, until finally she told my brother Bill and me.

She was afraid Bill and I would be upset. We weren't. In fact, we both thought it was pretty cool.

Unlike many of the young people with whom we grew up, we actually read books. It was a habit my mother, who taught us how to read before we entered school, encouraged and promoted. So we knew a little bit about history and the nature of the world.

We had our own stereotypical notion about Jewish people – a stereotype that has some factual basis. Jews are smart. Since they often were discriminated against, they couldn't rely just on material wealth, which could be confiscated, but they nurtured their mental proficiencies and skills.

Another reason Jews tend to be smart is that the dumb ones –

68

the ones that failed to pay attention – often ended up dying before they could pass their dumb genes on to a new generation.

Is that true? I really don't know if it is or not. We all believe what we want to believe, and that's how my brother and I responded to the news.

The sad kicker to my mother's story was that after War II, when my mother was married to my father and had her own household, two people came knocking on her door. They were from New York City and they were trying to track down a child who had been abducted years earlier.

Was she that child, now all grown up?

My grandfather was still alive, ailing and living in a Veteran's hospital. If he was found to have kidnapped my mother, there would be consequences. My mother made a quick decision.

No, she told them. You've got me confused with somebody else.

They turned and walked away, taking with them my mother's last chance to reconnect with my grandmother's side of the family.

Did my mother regret that moment? I don't think so. She made a decision, then she lived with it and moved on with her life. That's who my mother was.

It was one of the many things I loved and admired about her. And one of the many things I miss.

# The Tough Old Woman I Adored

### George – April 7, 1997

I have nothing clever to say. The woman who bore me, who raised me, who paddled my butt when I needed it, who taught me the difference between right and wrong, who made me appreciate the virtue of hard work and hard workers, and who instilled in me a stubborn pride that sometimes gets me in trouble, and a sense of humor that helps me keep those times in perspective, is fighting for her life in a hospital room in Florida.

My mother is a tough old woman from a generation of tough people – people raised during a great economic depression, tempered by a great war, who remain in their old age, proud of their strength and their country.

She is no stranger to death. Death has claimed two of her husbands and one of her sons, and someday it will take her too. I know this, but the little voice that lives within me keeps screaming: Not yet. Not this time. Just a few more years to visit and laugh and learn from this extraordinary woman who has already given me so much.

### April 14, 1997

When I was a kid, 8 or 9 years old, I thought getting a tattoo someday would be extremely cool. It would kind of say: Here's a real tough guy. Don't mess with him. I must have mentioned this to my mom, because she gave me some wise advice.

"Don't ever get a tattoo," she told me. "What if you decide to rob a bank? The police will have a sure way to identify you."

Now I suppose my mom could have said that a tattoo would make it hard to get into medical school, or that someday I would meet the girl of my dreams, and she wouldn't like a guy with a tattoo. But no, my mom just seemed concerned about the bank robbery angle. I never forgot her advice. Years later, when other guys were getting tough-guy tattoos, I abstained. It wasn't that I ever planned to rob a bank. I just sort of I wanted to keep my options open.

70

I told this story to Carmela, and the next time she saw my mom, she asked her about it. My mom never changed expression.

"You have to understand," she told Carmela. "I had to be both mother and father to the boys."

As far as my mom was concerned, that explained it all.

## June 24, 2002

Florence Georgine Davis, born in 1918, was a tough old woman from a tough generation.

She was not a complicated person. She cooked our meals, bandaged our cuts and abrasions, and made sure we knew the difference between right and wrong. She never read a book on how to raise a child. She just did it. She never discussed why we should do what she said. She just hugged us up when we did and slapped our fannies when we didn't.

But even tough people die. It's not just the congestive heart failure or the falls that become more and more frequent, or the shortness of breath or finally the violent seizures that suddenly come out of nowhere. It's all those things that in the end take their cumulative toll.

My mother died Friday evening, just two weeks shy of her 84th birthday. Carmela and I are in shock. By all accounts, her passing was peaceful. We didn't get a chance to say good-bye, at least not in person. But that's OK. We had the great good fortune to tell her how much we loved her many times over the past five years.

Five years ago, my mother spent several weeks in intensive care, and even the most dedicated doctors had given up hope. But that time my mother prevailed. This time she did not.

My mother died without regrets. She did not have an easy life, but she was feisty and happy to the end. She loved to sing old songs and laugh at the old stories. She was befuddled by modern stuff, from touch-tone phones to VCRs. And she never backed down from a fight.

She's been gone less than two hours, and we miss her already.

# My Boy's Mother

Carmela – May 7, 2007

The first time I met the woman who would eventually become my mother-in-law, I spent days scrubbing my apartment, cooking all kinds of goodies, and primping so I'd look just perfect. When Flo walked in the door, she looked pointedly at the floor and asked if I owned a vacuum cleaner. Three days later she told me she was "a little tired of Italian food," and in between, she talked

about how my future sister-in-law had all of her suits custom-made.

That first visit set the tone for the next 20 years. At some times we were so locked in struggle over who was in charge of the man that we both loved that I feared he would walk out the door and never return.

But it wasn't always that way. There were the nights that we'd listen to Rosemary Clooney and the Mills Brothers while we played Rummy 500, and the days that started with a strong pot of coffee early in the morning and ended at that same table – six strong pots of coffee later – long after dark. That's when I learned all about "Corky" and his brothers and what life was like for the young wife of a soldier who went to war for four years.

My mother-in-law was a strong and willful woman, and it took me some time to realize that the reason she and I fought – and perhaps the reason that her son married me – was that she and I were so much alike.

My mother-in-law died five years ago, and I miss that stubborn old woman. Sometimes I think of the hard time I gave her and of the times we'd battle, and I wish that I had told her thank you for the fine son she raised and that I loved her. And then I remember that I did tell her.

I only wish I had the chance to tell her one more time.

# The End of the Line

George – October 23, 2019

My mother's father, George Davis, grew up in Wales with a strong-hearted mother who apprenticed him out at an early age to a commercial artist. My grandfather's job was to paint pinstripes on horse-drawn carriages.

He ran away at 13, stowed away on a ship and ended up being a cabin boy until the ship landed near a rubber plantation in Brazil. There he quickly became an overseer, going on horseback from one outpost to another checking on native workers and looking after the owner's interests.

He never returned to Wales or to the family of his birth.

Or so I've been told.

My grandfather was still a young man when he later came to America, enlisted in the Army, and returned to Europe to fight the Germans. It was during the trench warfare that ensued that he was exposed to mustard gas, a chemical weapon used by the Germans that caused debilitating nerve damage.

Upon his return to the United States, my grandfather got a job as a commercial artist and married a woman who bore him a daughter. That woman was my grandmother, and her daughter was my mother. My grandfather later abducted my mother and raised her in Florida. He never remarried or had any other children.

My mother never connected with her maternal family again.

My mother dropped out of high school to marry my father when she was 17, a union encouraged by my grandfather who had been informed by doctors that he was dying as the result of progressive damage from his encounter with the poison gas.

With that in mind, he wanted to make sure there would be some young man to take care of his daughter. It was an old-fashioned concept, but he was an old-fashioned man.

I was born five years later, when my mother was 22, after an earlier pregnancy ended in a miscarriage.

My mother would sometimes talk about my birth and the panic she felt at becoming a mom. How do you take care of a baby, she asked the doctor that delivered me? What am I supposed to do?

He assured her that she just needed to take me home, love me, feed me and the rest would come naturally. And it worked, I suspect more from the resolve and inner strength that was a natural part of my mother's nature than from the doctor's advice.

My mother did not pour over books written by experts on child care and rearing. Thank God for that. She just did what came naturally.

She had two sons after me – Charles Kenneth Cunningham, better known as C.K. and later as Chuck – and William Patrick Cunningham, who went by Bill or Willie.

My brothers and I were very different people, in part because of the order of our birth, but mostly because of our inborn personalities. In the nature vs. nurture debate, nature always triumphs.

As the oldest, I was the responsible one. Hard working and dependable, but also a day dreamer who was easily distracted.

Chuck, six years younger, was a prankster, a drinker, a lover of women, and an adventurer. A little lazy sometimes, but never when the object was to have some fun. He was a soldier who served in Vietnam, a seaman on a ship, a brawler, a practical joker, and a loving brother. He loved women, but never enough to commit to just one.

If truth be known, he was the favorite brother of both myself and my brother Bill. He died in 1970 at age 23. He had no children.

Bill, eight years younger than I, was a hard worker and a salesman. He was one of those guys who was always closing a deal. Brave, brash, aggressive, and loving. A dominant force and a generous man in a world that longs for both domination and generosity.

None of my mother's sons felt compelled by any particular loyalty to the common wisdom or the social contract between state and citizen. We would obey the law when it made sense, and break it when it didn't.

Bill was smarter, braver, and a nicer person than I am. We would discuss a subject, analyze what was going on, agree on the facts right down the line, and then arrive at completely opposite conclusions.

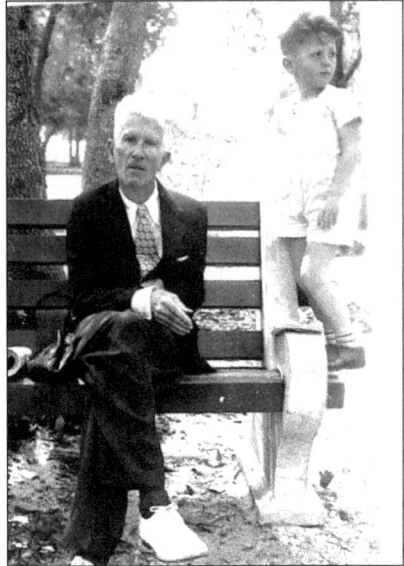

I loved my brother, but I was always right in how I saw the world, and he was almost always wrong.

My little brother died in 2014 at 66 years old after years of adventure on both sides of the law. He left a broken-hearted wife, but no children.

And that leaves me.

I was the eldest child. Never in my imagination did I think that I would be the only surviving son. I am now 79 years old, childless and closing in on 80, the last of a line that started with George Davis, my mother, and me.

As compensation, I have a string of nieces, nephews, brothers, and sisters that I have inherited as part of my marriage to Carmela Castorina, now Carmela Cunningham. But none from my side of the marriage. And that's OK.

It's not as much about who I am survived by, as it is about being the last survivor and missing those I loved, who shuffled off this one-way boulevard of life way before their time. I miss my mother and I miss my brothers. I even miss my father, although it ended badly with him.

As long as I'm alive, so are they, if only in my thoughts and dreams. I have no illusions that we will all meet up again, whether in Heaven or in Hell. But just in case I am wrong – and I have been wrong many times before – the reunion is sure to be a joyous and beautiful affair.

If that's the case, I can hardly wait for Carmela to join us too.

# Charles "Chuck" Cunningham, Better Known as "C.K."

George – August 18, 2020

My brother led a full life.

He fought in a war, he worked on a merchant ship as a seaman, he loved women, and they loved him. He was arrested at one point for rape, then released after the woman tearfully confessed that she had lied after her husband caught her and my brother in the act. He brawled in the streets, he was absolutely vicious in a fight, he pulled stupid pranks, he drank like a fish. He could be brutal, kind, foolish, and absolutely one of the funniest people I have ever met.

He was 23 years old when he died in a construction accident in 1970, and I mourn him to this day.

I was 5 years old, closing in on 6, when my brother arrived home from the hospital, and he was a trouble-maker from the first day. He was a so-called blue baby, a condition where his skin had a bluish tint, indicating a low level of oxygen in the blood. In most cases newborn infants overcome the condition, but my parents were worried because it could also be an indication of more serious heart problems.

My brother soon gave them something more to worry about. He loved making trouble. Early on he discovered that if he dropped his bottle out of his crib, somebody would come, pick it up, and pay attention to him. It was a typical scheme. He would drop the bottle, and my mother would pick it up and fuss over him. But as soon as she turned her back, he would throw the bottle back out of the crib in a bid for more attention.

Sadly, he overplayed his hand. My mother was most amused, but she wasn't about to encourage such behavior. Happily, he was

77

just learning to perfect his technique. He liked playing jokes and he liked manipulating people to see what would happen next.

It wasn't the only technique he was manipulating. He liked testing people, looking for the answer to the question: If I did blah-blah-blah, I wonder how people would respond. It was really comical sometimes, and sometimes a little ugly. But that was Chuck.

And as always with jokers, there were some tragic elements fueling the humor.

My brother Chuck grew up fast. I don't just mean he had a lot of grownup experience for his age, but physically he was remarkably tall – 6-foot-4 in fifth grade. It made him look like somebody who had flunked out numerous times and was still stuck in elementary school when he should have been in high school.

But looks were deceiving. Sitting at the little-kid school desk, it might have seemed as though he should have been in high school, but he was still just 11 years old. He entered sixth grade at 6-foot-5, and never grew another inch.

As I may have mentioned, my brothers and I all tended to have smart mouths, so we weren't all that popular with teachers. And we tended to get into trouble.

I was the oldest and the most responsible one. I worked my butt off from the time I was in elementary school to the time I was grown. Chuck was the joker. He didn't like work, and he had no problem with laying back and enjoying life. Our youngest brother Bill worked incredibly hard, but only if he was going to be paid for it.

If I liked a person, I tended to help them out for free, and sometimes people took advantage of that generosity.  Bill worked every bit as hard as I did, and often harder, but at the end of the job, he wanted money.

Chuck didn't like work.

He worked only enough to earn what he needed. He liked having fun and when you were with him, you ended up having fun too.  It made him a very popular and sometimes feared young man.

Chuck didn't like school. He didn't like the ring-the-bell and change-class regimen, the audacity of teachers who controlled what he studied and for how long, or the general silly nonsense that accompanied the whole production.

When he was 17, and I was 23 we joined the Army together. The date was January 13, 1964 – just eight weeks after President John F. Kennedy was assassinated. We got on a bus, spent the first night in a hotel in Jacksonville, Fla., then the next day rode to Fort Jackson, South Carolina for basic training, arriving late at night to a group of non-coms screaming at us to get out of the bus and line up for some late-night abuse. We were marched through a warehouse, had boots and fatigues thrown at us, had our hair buzz-cut down to the scalp, and made to understand that we were the lowest scum of the earth.

We were in the Army.

The discipline in the Army didn't bother Chuck as much as the discipline in school did. For one thing, we got to shoot at people-shaped targets with rifles, pistols, and machine guns, crawl under barbed wire while bullets were fired over our heads, throw hand-grenades, sleep in tents, learn hand-to-hand combat skills like how to use a bayonet or take down a sentry from behind, and have a rollicking good time getting to know other young men like ourselves.

Since it was January, we were often cold. We would have to get up in the middle of the night to do a shift shoveling coal into the furnace that heated our barracks. We would start our morning with calisthenics, go for a morning run on a route that always ended with a weary climb up "Drag Ass Hill," and then have a huge breakfast served on metal trays.

People would complain about the Army food, but Chuck and I had never eaten so well in our lives, and we could have as much as we wanted. And not-so-slowly, we began to get into good shape, enjoying the energy, discipline, and strength that young men need to assert themselves.

From there we went to advanced infantry training at Fort Dix, N. J., which meant on weekends, we were free to grab a Greyhound Bus to New York City to have fun, get drunk, and raise general hell. After Fort Dix, I went to jump school in Fort Benning to become a paratrooper, and Chuck went to Korea, where he served along the Demilitarized Zone that separates South Korea from the Communist North. I ended up in Okinawa with the 173rd Airborne Brigade.

The next time I saw Chuck was in 1965, when we both got emergency leave to return home because our father was dying. While I was home on leave, the 173rd shipped out from Okinawa to Vietnam. Chuck was reassigned also, ending up in Vietnam where he was attached as support to a Special Forces Group near the Mekong Delta.

Neither of us ever spent our time telling war stories, but Vietnam changed both of us. I was in a unit, living in a big rat-infested tent, surrounded by sandbags to stop shrapnel in case of a mortar attack. Chuck's unit was stationed as advisors to a South Vietnamese unit, where they interrogated Viet Cong and North Vietnamese prisoners.

Interrogation was a politically correct word for torture. On one of the rare times we did talk about Vietnam, Chuck told me how he could hear the prisoners screaming from where he slept. The screams drove him crazy, he told me. He finally stole pain-killers from the medical supplies and began giving them secretly to prisoners – an offense that would have gotten him court-martialed if he had been caught.

He was 19 years old at the time, but I believe the screams of the prisoners haunted him until the day he died.

My brother should have been an actor. He loved pranks, he loved make-believe, and he loved getting in trouble – whether it was fist-fighting, small-time thievery, or having too good a time. He would make up stories and act them out for his victims. And although he was only in his early 20s, he convinced people he was older by acting older.

For a while, he wore an earring – at a time before it was common for men to do so – and when people asked him about it, he told a story about how his unit had been wiped out in the war and only six men survived, and they all swore to wear an earring in one ear to remember their fallen buddies.

The person to whom he was telling the story usually ended up buying him a drink to hear the rest of the tale.

Another time, he found a clerical supply house that sold him a priest collar that he would wear out drinking. When he met a woman at the bar, they would have a conversation that always ended with him asking her to come back to his room. When she was shocked, he would tell her, "I'm a priest my dear, but I'm also a man."

I don't really know how successful this was at picking up women, but it was great fun as a joke.

On one occasion, he put on the collar, got a bottle of booze and laid in the gutter across the street from a Catholic church, swigging from the bottle and calling out "God Bless You" to all the faithful arriving for Sunday service.

Chuck worked for a while as a late-night bartender at Marineland, when it was located at the tip of the Palos Verdes Peninsula. The bar and restaurant were separate from the aquarium site itself.

The Peninsula area was being developed at the time with expensive homes overlooking the ocean. People buying the houses were often straining to make the payments. Chuck would get off shift around midnight, come home, and act out his customer's drunken laments, slurring his words as they did when they told him their troubles.

"Let me tell ya something, Chuck. Ima goddamn $25,000 a

year man, and I can't even afford to buy a goddamn palm tree for my goddamn front yard," my brother would relate. And by the time he finished with his stories about his customer's troubles, we'd all be laughing so much our bellies hurt.

He soon got a reputation of serving the driest martinis in the area. His secret, he told me, was not to put any vermouth in the drink at all, just pretend he was doing so. The customers, drinking straight gin with an olive in it, were delighted.

His love of practical jokes continued. He loved the Steve McQueen movie the Great Escape, where somebody used a cigarette as a slow-motion- fuse to set off an explosion. He decided to try it himself.

Around the Fourth of July, he bought a bunch of fireworks, gathered them into a big bundle on the front steps of the Palos Verdes Estates police building, lit the cigarette fuse, then went to a payphone down the street to call the station with a bomb threat and watch what happened next.

When the fireworks went off, the cops came running out of the station with their guns drawn, thinking they were under attack. He told us the whole story, acting out the cops' reactions and laughing so hard he had tears in his eyes.

One of the best parts of Chuck working at the Marineland restaurant was that after his shift ended, he would gather a bundle of steaks and lobster out of the restaurant's refrigerator, bring them home, and we would all eat like kings.

The scheme came apart after it became apparent that somebody at the restaurant was stealing cash from the drawer, and they required everybody who handled cash to take a lie detector test. One of the questions was have you ever stolen anything from the restaurant. Chuck said no and flunked the test.

To his way of thinking, stealing food to eat when he got home wasn't the same as stealing cash – but he got fired anyway.

Chuck took his dismissal in good spirits, but vowed to get even.

He phoned a florist, put on his best sad voice, and said he worked at the Marineland Restaurant and that the manager had died and that they were shutting down the restaurant at noon for a memorial service. He ordered a huge funeral wreath with a banner that said in "In Memory of Mr. (the name of the manager)." He charged it to the restaurant.

The wreath arrived along with the regular lunch crowd. Chuck had left the building, but his spirit remained behind.

Chuck worked for a while as a merchant seaman – part of the National Maritimes Union – an East Coast outfit that as middlemen, sometimes exploited their members as well as the employers. Before he shipped out, he had to go through a training period. One of the early steps was to go to a clinic to donate a pint of blood.

He later found out that he and the others were doing the donating, but the union man in charge was getting paid by the pint.

That didn't bother Chuck all that much. He was young, but he understood that the world is corrupt. What did bother him was actually working on a ship. It was boring and mind-numbing. After a couple of voyages, he decided to seek other employment.

Chuck was working on a dredging rig in Boca Ciega Bay with our friend Ron Sherrill when a rusted cable snapped, whipped around and slammed him in the head. He was dead, they said, before he hit the water. Ron was like a fourth brother, always hanging around our house, having fun, and getting into trouble.

Afterwards, the company sent a big bouquet of flowers, a sympathy card, and his last paycheck to our home. My brother had

no wife, no dependent children, and no family he was supporting. I wasn't surprised. I had worked construction myself, and seen people injured on the job and observed management's response – more interested in lost productivity than the human tragedy.

We were his family. We weren't looking for a big payout or any payout at all. We wanted the company to stop using old rusty, defective cables on their dredges and to take more precautions with the safety of their employees on what was already a dangerous job.

My brother was killed on June, 17, 1970. Six months and 12 days later, President Richard M. Nixon signed into law establishment of the Occupational Safety and Health Administration – an agency charged with protecting workers from unsafe practices.

I know Chuck's death was not directly responsible for the

legislation, but he and a lot of workers like him who had been injured or killed on the job, were the reason for the establishment of the new agency.

And that was better than any big monetary settlement from the company.

# The Softest Tough Guy I Ever Knew

Carmela – June 21, 2020

There are some people you get to know long before you meet them. They're the people whose stories precede them. Willie's stories always preceded him. The funny ones. The heroic ones. The tragic ones. The "what a jerk" ones.

Before I ever met Willie, I knew that he was an obnoxious little kid who always reeked of peanut butter and challenged his school teachers with the information he got every morning when his big brother read him the newspaper. I knew that by the time he was a teen, he was working and getting into fights and sleeping with girls. I knew about the time that he and his best pal Ron Sherrill were working as garbage men and a woman came outside with her little son and called them over.

"See," she said to her son pointing at Willie and Ron, "if you don't go to school and do a good job, you're going to end up like these two – garbage men! You don't want to be a garbage man, do you?"

And then one day I met him.

George and I had driven to Galveston to meet Willie, who had spent a few years in Texas during the oil boom, sometimes as a tug boat captain and sometimes as proprietor of a bar called "Fat Willie's." Willie's latest adventure was that he had bought the Louise Pearl, a beat-up "lightner" – a boat that was used to bring supplies out to anchored tankers. His plan was to clean up the Louise Pearl and take it back home. George was going to make the three-day voyage from Galveston to St. Pete, Florida with Willie, after a week of work on the boat.

We got into Galveston after dark, and we met Willie at a bar. I was nervous at first. I'd heard so much about him, but I'd never met him. Willie and George did not hug each other when they saw each other, even though it had been a few years. Neither were that kind of guy. We sat in the bar and ate. We drank and we talked. Hours went by. Even though the brothers had so much to say to each other, they're both Southern boys, which meant they left lots of space for me to talk too. I was working in aerospace at the time and told a few stories about the B-1B bomber. Willie listened intently, but every time I finished a story, he'd look at George and say, "is that right?"

"No Willie – I'm lying," I finally said.

Willie held the door open for me as George and I got in the car. I kissed him good night, and he closed the door.

"Did you just kiss my brother," George asked. "Yes," I said.

The next morning, we went to the place Willie was sharing with a couple other guys. He was in his tighty-whiteys and I made fun of him. We went to the boat yard, and as George and Willie and a few of his buddies worked on the outside of the Louise Pearl, I scrubbed and cleaned the inside. We worked for days. When she was all trim and clean and ready to go, they cut off her hull to replace it with some material Willie had just salvaged. It was going to make the Louise Pearl "a lot faster." It didn't. And it also took another week to get the hull back on. George and Willie finally took off for their three-day boat adventure and I flew home.

It took more than a week for them to get to Florida. During the time, they stole an anchor, one of George's two pairs of pants, which was being used for a sail, flew over the side. They put filters in backwards. They fought. They had a grand time.

Willie was always an adventure. Over the years, George and I took many trips to Florida. Willie would take me alligator-hunting at night, dragging a big spotlight down to lakes and gullies to shine in the water, looking for the tell-tale pair of eyes. We went fishing and scalloping and horse-back riding and lawn-mowing. For a time, Willie and his wife Susan had 40 acres and horses up near Tallahassee. He had one of those ride-on lawn mowers and he'd power it up, and I'd get on and make big figure eights in the horse pasture. We'd fight over the crossword puzzle and he'd tease me so much I'd get pissed off and sulk for days.

And then there was Dixie – a 140-pound Boerboel, who looked like she would rip your throat out, but was the most gentle dog I've ever known. Dixie was typical for Willie. A huge animal that was perfectly trained. Willie had a four-foot-high fence around the property. Dixie could jump it without blinking. Dixie could eat the fence if she wanted to. I was intimidated at first staring into those yellow eyes, but the second Willie introduced her to me, Dixie

85

became my protector too. We'd wander the pastures, and I'd love her up.

On our next visit a year later, we drove up to that little fence. Dixie came loping up, and I wondered if she'd remember me. I hesitated as I opened the gate, but Dixie took one look and rolled over so I could rub her tummy just like I had the year before. Dixie was Willie's dog. She hadn't forgotten me.

One time when Willie was out visiting us, George had gone to bed and Willie and I sat up talking for hours. We finally fell asleep on the living room floor. The next day, he took me riding on his motorcycle, which he had driven across country. We stopped at a store on the way back, and he bought a half-gallon of Chocolate Chip Cookie Dough ice cream. I'd never tasted it before. Willie and I stood at my kitchen counter with dueling spoons, eating ice cream out of the carton and fighting over the little pieces of cookie dough.

George and Willie and I worked together to rehab a house in Mount Washington. It was like those old cartoons where Donald Duck and his nephews build a house and everything is a disaster. But the three of us worked our butts off. We gutted the kitchen and took down a wall. We painted and tiled and carpeted and replaced toilets and sinks. There was a huge deck that jutted out about 30 feet over the ground. We took it down to 12-foot-long joists and Willie and I would crawl out on those joists like it was nothing. George went nuts. After a few weeks, we had rebuilt a slatted redwood railing on the deck and we spent days using Thompson's Water Seal to finish it. On the 4th of July, the three of us sat – filthy and stinking – out on that deck, watching fireworks and grilling steaks on a tiny hibachi.

At one point, George and I decided to get married. Willie was the best man, of course. I had this idea that I wanted them, and Larry, who was George's "second," not to wear tuxedos. I wanted them to wear "puffy, pirate, poet" shirts. Each of the men had their wives make their shirts.

The day before we got married Willie arrived from Florida. We

86

were stringing Christmas lights and I was cooking a meal for a bunch of my family who were coming over that night and trying to get things ready for the wedding. The day kept getting tenser and finally George and Willie fled to change the oil in our car. They came back a few hours later, and Willie came in and told me they had a little problem with the oil change.

"We're going to need to put a 'small hole' in the hood of the car," he said.

"How small?" I wanted to know.

"Well, big enough to fit my hand through. But look," he said. "I bought you a staple gun."

The day got worse. I got madder.

Late that night, after all my family left, Willie came out to model his puffy, pirate, poet shirt.

"Don't laugh" he said hiding on the other side of the door.

"I won't laugh," I promised.

Willie walked through the door looking like Sir Francis Drake with a belly. George and I both fell to the floor laughing so hard neither of us could get up. Every time we'd stop laughing and start to climb to our knees, we'd take another look and fall down again.

Willie did wear the shirt, although the minute the ceremony was over, he put a sports coat over it and refused to take it off.

Willie didn't toast us at our wedding. Larry later told us that Willie had written a toast and practiced it for several hours. But, when the moment came, Willie said he just couldn't do it.

Larry repeated some of what Willie had practiced.

"To the big brother who acted like my father, and to the sister I never had before," he started.

Willie was softest tough guy I ever knew.

When we lost Willie, the Good Lord gave us the gift of binding us into much tighter relationships with those who shared the loss. Our sister-in-law Susan. Willie's best boyhood friend Ron. Cousins George hadn't seen in decades, Roger and Nancy.

My brother-in-law was fearless about everything in the world. The only time I ever saw him scared is when he thought about losing one of the people he loved. He would risk himself on a daily basis. He wanted those he loved to always be safe and careful.

I miss Willie every day. He was so unique, so out of control, so bull-headed, that I can't really say who he was. We used to fight until I thought George would slam our heads together like a couple of coconuts. He'd tease me as only a big brother can.

To this day, Chocolate Chip Cookie Dough is the only kind of ice cream I eat. And as good as it always tastes, it's never quite as good as it was standing in the kitchen eating it out of the carton with Willie.

# My Brother Bill Who Broke My Heart

### George – August 31, 2020

I wanted one thing from my kid brother William Patrick Cunningham, and he let me down. I was eight years older than Bill, he was the only one left from my immediate family, and I wanted him to come to my funeral.

I would call Bill, and we'd both talk about how busy we were and how we didn't have much time to chat, then we'd talk for an hour or more, laughing at what was happening in our lives, and arguing about how we saw the world.

The plan was, Carmela and I were going to finish a book we were writing for the Port of Long Beach, then we were going to move to Florida, join Bill in the house he and our sister-in-law Susan Tucker were renovating in Seminole, and spend our days writing. It was a good plan and we were looking forward to the next phase of our lives.

Then in late October, I called Bill for one of our marathon chats, but he was late for an appointment and had no time to talk. But, before he hung up, there was a little pause on the phone and he said. "I love you, George."

I didn't grow up in a family with lots of hugging and emotion. Our love for one another was understood, but never said out loud. My brother had never said such a thing, not when we were kids or ever. Nor had I.

"I love you too," I finally said.

They were the last words we ever said to one another.

A few weeks later, on November 7, 2014, my brother died of a heart attack.

I should have said screw the book the minute I hung up from that last phone call with my brother. I should have gotten on the next available plane and flown back to Florida. I should have confronted him in person and asked him what the hell was going on with all this "I love you" crap.

That's what I should have done. That's what I would have done. But no, I had a book to write. I was on a tight deadline and I was almost finished. So, I did none of that, and the consequences were that the next phone call I got from Florida was from my sister-in-law Susan saying my brother had collapsed and died.

Should have, could have, would have, but didn't, do what I should have seen needed to be done.

I would give every dime we made on that book, every dollar we have in the bank account, everything I possess, for one day with my dead brother, an hour, a minute, or just a few seconds to repeat the last four words I ever said to him.

About a year after Willie died, I visited the cemetery where his ashes are interred in a memorial wall, just a few feet from my mother's. I sat there full of regrets and overwhelmed with sadness, when a chameleon, one of those cute little lizards you find all over Florida, scampered over the wall, crawled down until it was right on the plaque marking where my brother's ashes were contained, and stopped, looking directly at me and cocking its head, as if to say, don't be so sad.

Do I think the slinky little lizard was a messenger from my dead brother? Of course not. I'm not an idiot. But still. I want to believe, and maybe I even do just a little bit.

And sometimes just a little bit is just enough.

# My High-Flying Uncle Hank

George – August 31, 2020

Of all my uncles, my uncle Henry George Cunningham was by far my favorite.

In fact, if truth be known, I liked him way more than I liked my own father, his older brother. My Uncle Hank was more interested in science and the world and very much more patient than my dad.

I know now, from age and experience, that it's a lot easier to be patient and indulgent with somebody else's kids than with your own, because somebody else's kids go home at the end of the visit. Carmela and I have taken great pleasure in spoiling nieces and nephews, filling them up with sugar, letting them play in the mud, laughing at their bad behavior, and then sending them home to their parents.

While my father and his other two younger brothers were slogging across Europe on the ground, my Uncle Hank was fighting the war at 25,000 feet over Germany as a tail gunner on a B-17 Flying Fortress. That's exactly what he was doing in 1943, when his plane was shot out of the skies.

The last attack had sent his plane on a twisted, blazing dive toward the ground. He tightened his parachute and scrambled to the exit, only to find some of his crewmates already there, trying to open the jammed door. He rammed into it with his entire weight and it popped open, allowing him and the others to bail out.

The missions over Germany were dangerous, and casualties were high. When my uncle and the others first arrived in England, they were told they would rotate back to the states to train new bomber crews after 15 missions. But that promised number grew higher as the weeks went by and the war became more intense.

My uncle had flown more than 35 missions and had many close calls when his plane was shot from the skies.

I remember as a wide-eyed kid, listening to him tell the story.

"Weren't you scared to jump out that high up?" I asked.

He gave me that kind of wise-uncle look that let me know I was asking a stupid question.

"The plane," he said slowly and emphatically, "was on fire."

I loved airplanes. When I grew up, my fantasy job was to be a pilot, flying an airplane across the skies, defending the homeland from its enemies. Just like my Uncle Hank.

But my Uncle Hank didn't tell me the whole story, because I was a child and I was his nephew. The total story – the story of what happened next – was far grimmer. Bailing out of a plane was only the beginning of what was to come.

Flyers had been trained not to pull their rip cord until they could see the windows in the houses below. Opening one's parachute too high up exposed the flyer to enemy ground fire for a longer period. Although my Uncle Hank did as trained, he was still drawing fire from the people below who were trying to kill him before he hit the ground.

The bullets missed him, but not his parachute, which sent him hurtling at ever-increasing speed toward the ground because of the lost lift. He slammed into the earth at an angle, injuring his tail bone and causing problems that would plague him throughout his life. He was immediately captured and sent to a German Prisoner of War camp.

He would spend the next 15 months as a prisoner, being shuttled from Stalag to Stalag as the German Army retreated before the allied onslaught.

"Prisoner Safe and Well"

"Mrs. Ernest L. Cunningham 3526 Seventeenth Avenue South was escorted to the meeting by a young, handsome and inquiring companion, her grandson, George Cunningham. Her son and his uncle, whom he said to resemble closely, is S. Sgt. Henry G. Cunningham, now being held in Germany. The family has received word that he is safe and well.

Mrs. L. Chauncey Brown, chairman of the Red Cross relief to War Prisoners Service, rested here a moment from duties of the very active meeting. As she sat beside young George Cunningham in the study of Mrs. Julia S. Dyke, was she perchance thinking of her own sturdy little grandson? George broke a way just at that moment to sample again the punch and cakes served by the Red Cross Canteen."

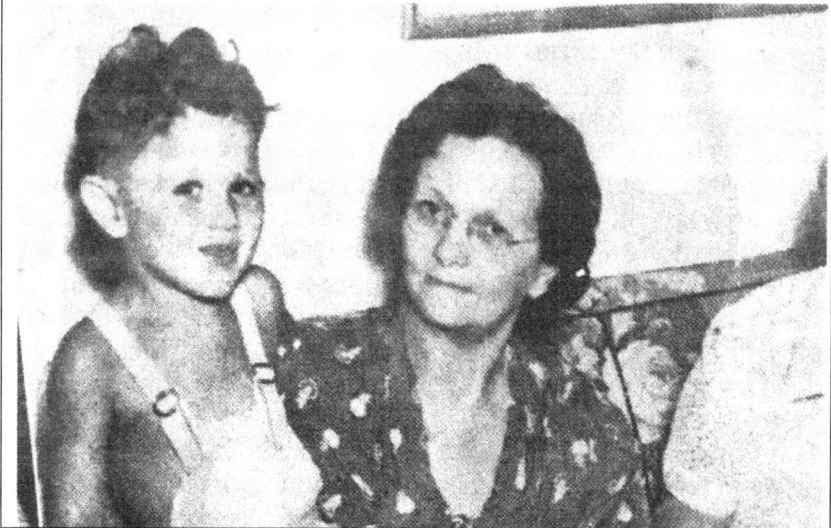

The movement from place to place, shackled together in cattle cars, was cold and brutal, leaving prisoners with no choice except to relieve themselves where they stood or squatted. When they came to places where the rails had been damaged, they had to hike to the next segment to get another train.

To drop out was to die.

With food running low for both guards and prisoners, the guards ate what little was available, and the prisoners scrounged what they could from the garbage, eating the peelings of carrots and other kitchen waste.

When he and the other starving POWs were finally liberated by Russian troops, they all had dreams of food, but bitter experience had taught that immediately satiating such craving often proved fatal. The released prisoners were shipped to Africa – it was winter in Germany – and introduced to food slowly, starting with broth and working their way to more hearty fare over a period of weeks.

Uncle Hank lost all of his teeth and suffered ongoing damage to his spine, but he prevailed – as many of his tough generation did.

My memories of my uncle were more than just his high-flying adventures in the skies over Nazi Germany or his capture and the time he spent as a Prisoner of War. Decades later I still remember his smell.

In the early days, my uncle worked as a coffee roaster preparing coffee beans for sale at Webb City – a huge department and grocery store in St. Petersburg – which advertised itself as the World's Most Unusual Drug Store. Webb City catered to both locals and tourists and featured such attractions as orange-blossom honey, a huge magazine stand with pinup magazines that drew young boys like myself, and a special section with "talking mermaids" that were merely mermaid manikins with women behind a screen chatting up visitors.

Among the special products offered at Webb City was the special Webb City coffee, with beans that were roasted by my Uncle Hank. And he smelled like what he did. He has been dead for many years, but to this day I can't smell coffee beans roasting without thinking of him.

He became quite efficient at the coffee business, understanding how to mix the beans to achieve the desired taste. The Webb City coffee brand later became part of the Eight O'clock Coffee line, which incorporated many of my Uncle Hank's blends into their lineup of offerings.

After my uncle left the coffee-roasting business, he went to work as a technician for Peninsula Telephone, which later became part of GTE and still later Verizon. I loved it because he would bring home books explaining how electricity worked, complete with little cartoon electrons flowing down a wire, connecting one place to another. From my uncle I learned about the difference between Alternating Current and Direct Current, how radio and television tubes worked, and the definition of voltage and amperage.

He married May Huff, whose family owned a plant nursery not far from where my grandparents lived. He and my Aunt May lived in a front house they built not far from her parents' home and my grandfather and grandmother lived in a garage apartment to the rear of the house.

Years later, after my father left, my mother and my brothers and I were on our own, and I no longer saw my Uncle Hank or the rest of my extended family. My mother and my brothers were the only family I had.

My uncle died in 1986 after being diagnosed with cancer. When the doctor asked if he had experienced any stress in his life, my uncle talked about the time during the war when he was shot out of the skies and almost starved before being liberated by allied troops. He was 65 years old when he died.

My Aunt May never remarried. She lived with her son, my cousin Mike, until 2013, when she passed away. She was 88.

I was not aware of their deaths until I reconnected with my extended family years later. They have kindly welcomed me back into the fold. What do we have in common?

Once in a while, you see my grandfather's sense of humor crop up or my uncles' curiosity about the world, or my grandmother's stubborn Baptist work ethic. But mostly just blood.

Sometimes, that's enough.

# The Day the Children Would Not Stop Crying

### Carmela – February 27, 2000

I never wanted to eulogize my mother. I did not know her long enough. I did not know her well enough. But there I was standing in front of family and friends, trying hard to say something that would sum up 80 years of a woman in less than 20 minutes.

My mother was many things to many people

To her sisters, she was a young woman of style and beauty, and an old woman of music and art. To her best friend and sister-in-law Joan, she was the perfect travel companion – and a good navigator. To my father, she was a wife.

To her children and the people who married her children, she was the mom. To her grandchildren, she was Nona.

My mother was beautiful and strong. She had lupus erythematosus in her late 40s, and although she managed to survive it at a time when it was considered fatal, the disease left her with kidney disease and heart problems. But that doesn't mean my mother was sickly or weak. She worked as a waitress for most of her life and raised my five siblings and me. She was the matriarch of our clan and the favorite of her grandchildren and nieces and nephews – all of whom remained close to her even as they became adults and had children of their own.

But by the time she turned 80, it all caught up with her. After a year of kidney dialysis, her body was ready to give it up. During the course of her last eight months, she spent three weeks in a nursing home. During those three weeks, she never had less than two visitors a day. One day she had 13 people in her room at the same time – daughters, grandkids, sisters, nieces and nephews. Later, in the main dining room, my mother played the piano, her sister Lil sang, the grandkids ran around eating cookies, and their mothers just shook their heads.

One Sunday George and I went to visit her. When we got there, my mother was sitting in her wheelchair. Her 14-year-old granddaughter Mallory was lying in the bed, using the remote to move the bed up and down. Seven-year-old Bailey was dealing a hand of poker, and 12-year-old Jillian was reading National Enquirer aloud to them all. They were eating Taco Bell.

Eventually we got my mom out of that nursing home, and she lived several more months. Those months were a gift of piano-playing, painting, ravioli-making with her grand - children,

and a last family Thanksgiving and Christmas.

But then one day in February, I sat in my mother's hospital room, watching as her oldest grandson, Erik, laid his strong arm next to her frail one, holding her hand as the nurse stuck a needle in her arm to hook up an IV. Two days later Death came, and when he left he took with him Pearl Reader Castorina. At the end she was surrounded by her children, her grandchildren, her first great-grandchild, nieces, nephews, and other members of her extended family who came to say good-bye

Death wears many faces. He can be horrible, he can be unspeakably cruel, and he can sometimes be kind. He is a teacher who leaves us all with a not-so-gentle lesson of what truly is important in life and truly what is not.

My mother's last months were not without pain. She was prodded and poked, her body invaded by instruments designed to buy her time. Three days a week she went to dialysis, where her blood was drained and cleaned and put back in her veins. She was often cold and sometimes in great discomfort. But she was also surrounded by family. She laughed, she gobbled down the Twix candy bars we brought her, she listened to music, and she even made sketches in her drawing pad.

Days before her death, she held her great-grandson and fed him spaghetti as she had done with her children, her grandchildren, her nieces and nephews. There was a constant stream of babies that flowed through my mother's life, and she always had time for each and every one. They loved her for that.

My mother left this world wrapped in the love of her children and grandchildren. At her memorial service, eight-year-old Olivia sat on my lap sobbing until I took the gold heart necklace that had been my mother's from around my neck and put it on hers. The older girls sat behinid me cuddling each other and crying uncontrollably. Her grandsons carried her to her final resting place with five-year-old Joe Buck walking in front of the casket, holding up a cross. He was helping take his Nona to Heaven and he was very brave and confident. Later that day he asked when we were going to go to Heaven to pick up Nona and bring her back home. It was harder for him then.

For months after we buried my mother, my sisters, my mother's grandkids, and I would go to "Nona's Stone" and have picnics. Jake and Joe would polish her stone, and the girls would place flowers and pinecones all around. We'd eat Taco Bell and finish it off with Twix bars. We'd always leave some for her.

There is no more pain for my mother. She is finally and forever at peace. No more turmoil or discomfort. No regrets or disappointments.

Death is gone for now, but he'll be back. We can't control that. All we can control is how we treat each other in the meantime.

# Silent Joe

George – November 21, 2020

Joe Castorina, my father-in-law, is a man.

A good man, a bad man, a selfish man, a giving man, a stubborn man, a tolerant man, a mean man, and a kind man. Joe Castorina is all those things, but most of all he is a man in the old-fashioned sense of what being a man is.

He was born in Sicily, but he grew up poor and hungry in New York during the depression, caught between two cultures, doing whatever was necessary to survive. He served in World War II – on board the battleship USS Nevada on D-Day in Europe as allied troops poured onto the beaches and the tide turned against Hitler. And he served aboard that same ship the following year as suicidal Kamikaze pilots flung their aircraft toward American ships in a last-ditch effort to stave off an allied victory.

Joe moved to California after the war – both because that's where his bride was from and to escape the Mafia culture in which he grew up.

He served as a Los Angeles Sheriff's deputy and as a detective. He had six children, two boys and four girls. As he had done his entire life, he did whatever he had to do to put food on the table for his family and himself.

When his wife grew gravely ill, he took a second job as a truck driver, coming home to take a quick nap, change clothes, yell at the kids, and go back to work. He was not a sensitive male – not then, not now. He was outspoken, pushy, often rude and used to plain talk.

His nickname when he worked as a Sheriff's Deputy was "Silent Joe." He was called Silent Joe because he liked to talk, and talk, and talk. But he also liked to watch and listen. His years in poverty and war, growing up in Little Italy where mobsters ran the neighborhood had taught him the importance of paying attention to what was going on around him.

It's called situational awareness. It's a valuable talent, not necessarily appreciated in today's world where people go to and from home and work and even leisure activities with earphones blasting music in their ears or texting others from across the country. People who float through life with little awareness of what is happening to the right or left or even right in front of them.

It was one of the things that made Joe a good detective. He could spot people acting suspiciously, people up to no good, people getting ready to take advantage of other people. He grew up in that kind of a world, and he was not afraid to confront people up to no good or to understand people who were caught up in a hostile culture.

Joe is no saint. He often made life hard on his wife and his children. But he was always there, fulfilling his obligations as a provider and protector. He was not a perfect man, but he was OK with that. He accepted his own imperfections without long-suffering pangs of guilt or shame.

Joe Castorina is a man of his time. He loves women, but he prefers the company of other men. At family gatherings, he will let the women talk about clothes or children or gossip about all the trivial concerns women have. But Joe always wants to hang out with the men.

He is not an understanding male, a guilt-ridden male, an insecure male, or a man made to feel ashamed of his masculinity. In other words, he is a man of his time – a time when being a man meant something in the world.

My father-in-law, Joe Castorina, is dying.

He is blind, almost deaf, and suffering from both pain and isolation.

Several years ago he told me that he planned to live to be 100. He is 99 and several months old as I write this, but the country covid shutdown may steal those last few weeks from him. He has been quarantined for months now and quarantine for a man like Joe is a slow death.

He grows weaker by the day. So weak that even those who love him wish for his ordeal to end. It will soon.

And the world will be a little less tough and a little more ugly after he is gone.

**EPILOGUE:** Joseph Castorina died on January 25, 2021. He had a pretty spectacular life for a kid born in Messina, who came to America as a very little boy and grew up in Brooklyn. He was a Navy Signalman and fought in World War II. He was a Deputy Sheriff for 30 years. He was also a truck driver, a security guard, and had a host of other jobs growing up. He was a husband, father, grandfather and great-grandfather. He was also a great story-teller.

# First Love and A Twice-Broken Heart
## Carmela - May 28, 2020

I have letters. Long and sweet and sad love letters. They're more than 45 years old now, and they sit in the top of my closet in an old plastic Weber's bread bag. I don't know why they're in a bread bag. They should be in a beautiful box with a big pink ribbon tying it closed.

The letters came from my very first real love, the one I would have married, the one that remains sweet and gentle in my heart.

Jon was a very tall, very principled, very smart young man. He was funny and kind and generous and made a wonderful person for me to fall in love with when I was 19. But he would not have been a good husband for me at all.

I met Jon in high school. He was a year older than me and the crush of my best friend. They never got together. He and I were much better suited. We both played chess and read poetry and went to classical music concerts. We talked philosophy, read literature and explored fabric stores in search of home decorating ideas. We were best friends, and somewhere along the way, we fell in love.

Jon was unusual, but that was OK, because I was too. He was a strict Mormon and had plans to go on a two-year mission after high school and two years of community college. After that, he'd go to Brigham Young University, where he'd get his bachelors, and master's degrees, and then a PhD. in Psychology. Then he would marry, move to Utah, and raise a very large family with his wife – with whom he'd spend time and all eternity.

It sounded good to me, so I converted. That's not as fickle as it sounds. I studied the church teachings – including more of the philosophy than most Mormons learn. I signed up for several volunteer jobs at our church ward and bore my testimony week after week.

We spent the two years after high school at Cerritos Community College, doing almost everything together. Mostly, we planned our future. I took up sewing, and Jon would go with me to pick out fabrics and patterns so I could make my own clothes. He'd hand me pins as I sewed. And we talked. And talked and talked. We took classes together, cooked together, listened to music, and went on dates. What we never did, was have sex. We were young and in love, but the Mormon church has strict guidelines, and we followed them.

Finally, it came time for Jon to leave on his two-year mission to Venezuela. As we said good-bye that last night, I started crying and by the time I got home, I was crying so hard I could barely speak. When I saw my mother, I sobbed, "Jon left." But I was crying so hard, she thought I said, "Jon died." It didn't matter what I had said. Jon was gone. And it broke my heart.

My two years waiting for my missionary to return began well. I got a job and continued at Cerritos, doing my own Psychology prep work to fulfill my own plans to go to BYU when Jon got back. I spent time with his parents and time coaching girls' basketball at the church.

For 18 months, I sent and received a letter every week. We kept dreaming and planning and even talked about getting married as soon as Jon got home – instead of waiting until we were both doctors and financially settled.

And then things changed – although I'm still not quite sure what – or even when. I started doing other things and the letters slowed down in both directions. I didn't date other people, and I still wanted all the same things – marriage, children, traveling and opening a practice together. But Jon and I just weren't clicking as much. When he finally got home, we got together a few times, but we both knew it was over. After all those years of talking, we never talked about why. We never acknowledged it was over. We just went our separate ways.

***

As I spend what would have been his 66th birthday looking through his letters, I believe Jon knew that he was gay all that time ago. Or maybe he just had feelings he couldn't understand. He loved me. He loved his church. He just couldn't figure out how to put it all together.

Eventually, I did marry, and so did Jon. And although I never met his husband, Jon did tell me that he was very principled and smart and funny and kind and generous. That made me happy.

A few years ago – after decades of losing touch - I found Jon on Facebook. We shared close to a year of "likes" and private messages before one day Jon's husband showed up on his Facebook page and told all of Jon's friends and family that Jon had died suddenly that morning. Jon was 62. His husband was heart-broken. So was I. For the second time.

Today I went to one of those big fabric stores Jon and I used to haunt, and I bought something they didn't carry 45 years ago. A big beautiful box with soft pink roses and muted purple dahlias all over it. It snaps closed, but there's also a big mauve bow to tie around the box.

Jon's letters are finally where they belong.

# My Pal: Larry LaRue 1949-2017

## George – November 29, 2017

Death always takes you by surprise. No matter how old the person is, no matter how frail they have become, no matter what the doctors say, when somebody you care about dies, it is always a surprise.

Not today, you think. Not now. Maybe next year, or next month, or even next week.

My friend Larry "Lash" LaRue died earlier this month, and I find myself at that place where I see something funny or outrageous, and I think, I've got to tell Lash about this. And then, it hits me that Lash is gone and he's not coming back.

And it hurts.

Lash and I knew each other for more than 40 years – longer than either of us had known our wives. We met at the Orange County Register. He was coming from a job as a reporter at the Omaha World Herald; I had been working at City News Service in downtown Los Angeles and before that at the Daily Breeze in Torrance.

We were very different people. The stories flowed from his brain through his finger tips and onto the printed page. I struggled more, agonizing over each word, often going back and changing sentence structure, trying to figure out how I wanted to tell the story and what were the important facts that needed to be in it.

I fought in the Vietnam War, he protested against it. I voted for Reagan, he voted for Carter. He loved sports; I couldn't care less.

Yet, we loved spending time together. The same things made us laugh, and the more outrageous, the better.

There was an editor at the Register who was among the stupidest people to ever walk the planet. This editor took all the writers who worked for him to lunch one day and gave us all grades. Larry and I both got C-minus, but it didn't make us mad. We found it hilarious. We gave the guy a nickname – "the incredible shrinking brain."

From then on we just called him the Brain – as in the "Brain" wants to know what stories we have coming for tomorrow's paper. We both knew the "Incredible Shrinking" part was understood.

We were out of control. We probably should have been fired, but we weren't. They had this thing at the Register where a big story would break and each reporter was expected to call five people on the phone to ask what they thought about it. So we'd get one of those assignments, and we would call the local massage parlor and ask the girls there what they thought about the latest Supreme Court decision. And they would always say stuff such as, "Is that like the Supremes – I love their music." Another time, we looked up the goofiest names in the phone book, so all our respondents had silly names like Harry Butternut or Betsy Pigg.

And through it all, everybody just shook their heads and let it go, because at the end of the day, we were both good writers at a time when that meant a lot in the newspaper business. Everybody in the business was goofy back then. We would go to lunch at some dark bar, have a few drinks, and walk out blinking at the sunshine about three hours later. The other side of the story was that we would still be hanging around at 9 that night, making phone calls and writing stories.

We both had guns and we would go out in the desert with our .22s and shoot at jackrabbits. The rabbits would run like crazy with the bullets kicking up dirt all around them, and we'd be laughing like mad men and shooting away, until we finally hit one of them and blew off most of his leg. So we went up and shot him to put him out of his misery. We gave up shooting at jack rabbits after that. We both realized we liked shooting at jack rabbits and scaring the Hell out of them, but hated actually hurting one of the little guys.

We did a lot of stupid things back then, things that I regret today. Things like racing through traffic, weaving in and out of lanes, just for the wild fun of it. One of those times, he was ahead of me as we neared our office, but I hopped the curb and went screaming and sliding across a vacant field to cut him off and I won. He was laughing so hard he could hardly stand up.

One of the more stupid things we did – or maybe I should say I did – was when Larry talked me into wrestling a bear at the Anaheim Convention Center for a story in the Orange County Register. I asked him why he didn't want to wrestle a bear, and he said he would like to, but he couldn't because of an old baseball injury from when he was in college.

He told me, don't worry, it's a black bear named Victor, weighs in at about 400 pounds, just tussle around with him and it will be fun. Well, after we set the whole thing up, it turned out that Victor the black bear had died and been replaced by Victor II, a bigger Alaskan brown bear that stood 8-foot-three and weighed 643 pounds.

We had a strategy. I was going to dance around, taunt the bear, maybe run around real fast and kick him in the butt, put on a show for the audience. Long story short – the bear kicked my ass, knocked me down, and fell on me. I was totally out of it, seeing stars, and bleeding from a cut on my forehead. Victor's trainer, a guy named Tuffy Truesdell, grabbed me, turned me around, and said, "the crowd loves it," as he pushed me back into the ring. Victor proceeded to do a repeat performance, while Larry stood by the ringside, grabbing pictures with his camera. It was on the front page of the paper the next day.

We also worked together in 1975 on two murder cases that revolved around the Playgirl Club in Garden Grove. The club had a shady past with hints of public corruption. Not only had the City Council rushed through an after-hours permit for the club, but council members frequented the club where they were given the VIP treatment. Rumors of ties to organized crime were hotly denied by the owners, and the after-hours permit was challenged by several gay nightclubs in Garden Grove that wanted equal treatment. For conservative Garden Grove in the 1970s, after-hours gay nightclubs were out of the question. The after-hours permit for the Playgirl Club was withdrawn as well.

It turned out the club was also a gathering place for off-duty cops and for an illegal weapons business involving machine guns and silencers. At least two people were murdered as part of a cover-up.

The paper wasn't really interested in sending a reporter all the way to San Bernardino to cover a trial – even if it did center on an Orange County nightclub. Lash and I would sneak out of work – Larry on one day, me on the next – one to go gather information and one to cover for the other.

The story turned out to be huge, involving both law enforcement incompetence and corruption. After showing up with stories about what had been going on at the Playgirl Club, we finally convinced editors it was worth the drive to San Bernardino.

One guy, an informant for federal Alcohol, Tobacco, and Firearms agents, was killed after he told ATF undercover investigators that he thought he was going to be murdered. ATF promised to protect him, then abandoned him out in the desert because their unmarked sedans made it impossible to follow the murderers' off-road vehicles into the desert without blowing their investigation.

And when the informant was murdered, nobody bothered to tell his family until his body was discovered more than two years later. When his wife had reported him missing, the Orange County Sheriff's detective – putting in his time until retirement – filed it and forgot it.

San Bernardino Sheriffs, who took over the case when one of the bodies was found in their jurisdiction, quickly nicknamed the ATF partners "Heckle and Jeckle."

At the end of the investigation, numerous cops were fired, including the main suspect's brother – an investigator with the Orange County Sheriff's Office – who had tipped off the suspect that the investigators were closing in.

Unfortunately, before all the writing was done, Lash – who was having problems at home and the office – got so pissed off that he quit his job and left his then-wife all on the same day. It was also the day that his cat died. It was never entirely clear which event pushed him over the edge, although I always suspected it was the cat.

Lash loved animals.

During the next few months, Lash worked as a private detective. He had a little compact Ford pickup with a camper shell and he would climb in the back to stake out suspects. Then during the day, he would go to his old alma mater, Cal State Long Beach, shoot some hoops in the gym, take a shower, and change his clothes.

We would meet up some times and tell each other stories and make each other laugh. Like the time he had staked out a Cadillac that had been repeatedly vandalized. After several nights and hours lying in the back and staring out camper shell windows, he saw the perpetrator throw a bag full of paint on the Caddy and run off.

Lash jumped out of the truck to chase him down, but his foot had fallen asleep, so he ended up limping after the guy, yelling for him to stop. Lucky for Lash, vandals aren't all that smart. The guy ran into his own apartment and locked the door.

Lash banged on the door and ordered the guy to come out. The guy may have been stupid, but he wasn't crazy. He stayed put, and the cops took over from there.

Larry and I also worked as an unofficial team covering the Skid Row Slasher in L.A., Larry laid in the doorway, posing as a bum, while I was staked out down the block with a .357 magnum snub-nosed revolver, covering his butt. The gun was not at all accurate beyond close range, but it made a Hell of a noise and shot a flame about six inches out the barrel that would light up a dark night and scare the bejesus out of any would-be assailants.

Another time, when I was about 50 and Larry was just getting started on his 40s, we decided it was time to go out and prove we still had what it takes to be tough guys, even though we were quite a bit older than we had been. We drove around, going to different bars, seeing if we could stir up a fist fight or at least a push-and-shove confrontation. If that sounds incredibly stupid, neither of us every claimed to be boy geniuses.

We went to a couple of Mexican bars along PCH, drank our cervezas, and tried to look tough. But nobody took the bait, so we finally went to a Navy bar up on Long Beach Boulevard, which had a reputation for violence, and went in and ordered a couple of beers. I had thick, curly hair at the time, and one of the drunks, came up, felt my head and said in a loud voice, "Oh man, I want to butt fuck the guy who does your hair." I pointed to Larry, who was sitting on the stool next to me, and said "here he is."

Larry almost fell off the stool laughing. The guy backed right down. Started telling us how he was just joking and all. Bottom line is, we went home a little tipsy, laughing our asses off as we usually did when we got together, and truthfully kind of pleased with ourselves.

Larry got into sports writing. He was covering the World Series in Candlestick Park in 1989, when the Loma Prieta earthquake hit San Francisco. Some of the eastern sports writers, who had never been in an earthquake, split for home. Larry switched from sports writer to reporter and began covering stories of the aftermath, writing about a family whose home was on the epicenter of the quake and about a homeless man who crawled up the side of a collapsed double-decked freeway to rescue trapped motorists.

Larry later wrote a book, which Carmela and I published, called Major League Encounters – talking about his experiences covering baseball. His anecdotes about the players and the coaches in that very elite world drew praise from all sides.

It was during his time as a sports writer that Larry was

diagnosed with diabetes. Unfortunately, he didn't take care of himself – especially traveling with the team, where it was difficult to maintain a proper diet.

Diabetes is a cruel disease, and it took its toll, both on his eyesight and his heart. He made it through his first heart attack – dying on the operating table before surgeons got his heart pumping again. Although he was eventually able to go back on the road with the Mariners, more cardiac and vision complications through the ensuing years left him fragile and frail.

Wives do whatever is necessary to keep their husbands alive and healthy, even if it means nagging, yelling, and lying to do so. And it works. But the sad truth is that wives can only do so much. Death always wins in the end. It's waiting for us all, the only question is when.

Death claimed Larry earlier this month.

Larry was a dear friend. Carmela and I went to lunch with him in Long Beach on a Saturday, two days before he died. After lunch, we went to drive him back to where he was staying, but ended up just driving around for more than an hour, talking about things, laughing as we always did when we got together, and making plans for when he would be back in town again from Gig Harbor, Washington, where he lived.

We both gave him a hug when we left, we told him that we loved him, and we were looking forward to seeing him again in a little more than a month.

I miss the boy. It's still hard to believe that he's gone. He's almost nine years younger than me, and he died way before he should have. He was a sweet man with a generous and loving spirit.

And he always knew how to make me laugh.

# The Last Time I saw Betsy

Carmela – March 29, 2020

I have to admit I was a little bit nervous when I first called Betsy. After all, I was 63 years old and planning to learn to play the piano. I had absolutely no musical ability whatsoever. If I had ever accidentally carried a tune, no one ever noticed it – least of all me. I couldn't read music, and I didn't know the keys on the piano. But it had been a dream since I was a child, and I had retrieved my mother's piano – the piano I had grown up with – from the desert, and it was sitting, tuned and ready to be played in my living room. All I needed was a piano teacher. And boy did I get one.

Earlier I had asked a couple who I had met in my new neighborhood if they knew a good piano teacher. "Betsy!" they both yelled at the same moment. I looked her up and gave her a call.

Betsy didn't answer the phone when I called. One of her caretaker/companions did. That was a bit odd to me, but I made an appointment to meet her. I dressed carefully for my first appointment – I wanted to make a good impression. And although I didn't cut my fingernails, I did worry that Betsy would tell me to do so. This was obviously an older lady, and I assumed she'd be like the old-lady piano teachers you see on TV. A big flowery dress draping extra-Rubenesque curves and falling to her ankles. A high, stern voice, and a task-master's set of rules that dictated short fingernails for pianists.

But that wasn't Betsy. Betsy was beautiful. She said she was 87, but she was really 92. She had been married four times – all to men she adored. She had a baby grand in her living room and everything around her house was elegant, arty and musical. Just like Betsy. She was dressed in a blue and white long-sleeved top with white cropped pants and blue shoes for our first lesson. Her bobbed platinum hair was perfect, and so was her make-up, which included more than a whisper of blue eye shadow on the lids of her huge blue eyes and a deep red slash of lipstick. Her fingernails were long and bright red and perfectly shaped.

"I love that blouse," she said when I walked in. "Why don't you give it to me?"

"I think it will scandalize the neighbors if I go home topless," I said.

"That's OK, she answered without blinking. They need to be scandalized." I got the feeling Betsy had scandalized a lot of people in her long life.

We started chatting. And then we started practicing. Sadly, Betsy's beautifully manicured hands were arthritic. She could show me notes to play, but she never actually played more than a few notes. Her bent and crippled hands wouldn't do that anymore.

As Betsy directed me, I scribbled notes in a journal. We began with the first book of "Piano Adventures" and started practicing piano greats such as "Zoom, Zoom the Witches Broom," and "Pterodactyls, Really Neat." It was a good first lesson.

I practiced all week, and when I went back, I had mastered "Zoom, Zoom" to the "painfully awful" level. I was worried Betsy was going to get after me. But she didn't.

She was in red and white and wore a blouse with a musical note on the front. And she was chatty. She started telling me stories that continued over the next months and painted the picture of an independent woman who did exactly what she wanted from the time she was a child.

She told me about how she had studied with Liberace's teacher, which had led to her meeting Liberace himself. She talked about traveling to Paris and playing the piano and arranging music. She said her older sister was mean and lazy, but she adored her brother. She had always loved beautiful clothes and she just couldn't stop dancing. At that point she'd stand up and take a twirl around the room in the arms of her invisible partner.

Her last husband was an artist, and his work hung throughout the house. Every morning when he was alive, they'd get up, eat breakfast, and then he'd go paint and she would practice the piano and arrange music.

She loved dogs, and her current was Jasmine – the last in a line of standard-size poodles. Betsy said Jasmine was perfectly trained and never did anything wrong, but I saw Jasmine steal cookies off the plate on the table all the time. Betsy had a bright red Solara convertible with a "Sonata" license plate. It was snappy and fast and cute. Just like Betsy. Betsy didn't actually drive her Solara anymore. But her companion drove her around in it.

I got caught up in Betsy's stories, and if there was a lot of repetition, that was OK. I loved her life, and I loved her.

As time went by and I got busy, I didn't practice as much as I should have and because she was slipping, I could dazzle Betsy with exactly the same thing I had learned the week before. Plus, we were both always willing to just chat about things. She'd ask what I was doing in life, and I'd ask her anything. She would tell me stories – often stories that she had told me before, but that I loved hearing again and again.

But then Betsy's health started declining. Jane, her caretaker would call and cancel for the week. And then she'd call and cancel "for a few weeks."

Then one week it happened. I showed up and Betsy was wearing pajamas and a robe with a piano keyboard embroidered on it. She sat in a wheelchair. She was so tiny and frail, but the second Jane left, Betsy told me, "get me out of this chair. I want to play with you."

Because her hands had been in such bad shape since I met her, Betsy never played those piano teacher duets with me, so I was surprised that this day she wanted to play.

I got her out of her chair, and we played "All I Ask of You," from Phantom of the Opera. We were on the second round when Jane came back and was horrified that I had gotten Betsy out of her chair. I helped Jane get Betsy into bed and said my good-byes.

Later that week Jane called and said Betsy was going to need a couple weeks off and it might be better if they called to tell me when Betsy was ready again. It broke my heart, because by then I knew that Betsy would never be ready for another lesson. Weeks and then months went by. They put Betsy to bed and there she laid, not really communicating and not having visitors. Then one day, I got the notice that I knew would come. Betsy finally let go of the wonderful life that she had loved so much.

I'd like to tell you that after my time with Betsy, I'm a beautiful piano player. But I'm not. I play like Frankenstein. Hands hovering over the keys - like they're part of a computer keyboard - squinting at the notes in my old lady glasses. Yelling to no one in particular – it's a G! A G you idiot! You know the G! You like the G! It's a fucking G!

If you think Betsy would be offended by that language, you're wrong. She was the most elegant, accomplished, lovely lady I've ever known. But even better than that, she was such a hoot.

# TOMBSTONE TERRITORY

George – January 16, 2019

Do the dead hold grudges?

I hope not. I hope that after folks have passed on, all the grievances and the differences that separated them in life are buried along with the physical bodies they no longer need.

But it's hard to say, especially in a small town like Ely, Nevada, where friends and enemies in life end up just a few feet from one another, buried beneath the gravely surface in coffins separated only by dirt and the roots of tall trees. Some of the dead have fancy stones above their graves, others have more simple plaques, but financial or social status doesn't mean that much when you're dead.

The Ely City Cemetery is small – unlike the Forest Lawn or Rose Hills or Arlington mega-cemeteries of Southern California. The graves come down almost to the sidewalk along busy E. Aultman Street, separated only by a 30-inch-high rock wall. Across the street is the Big 8 Tire Store and the Cruise-In Car Wash and Mini Lube.

Most of the graves at the Ely cemetery are actual upright stones – not the little flat plaques in the ground that make it easier to mow the grass and keep down maintenance costs, as is common in newer big-city plots. The upright stones make it quicker to locate the graves of loved ones and gives each grave a little personal style of the person or persons buried beneath.

Except for the sound of nearby traffic, the Ely cemetery is blissfully calm on a weekday morning. Aultman is a busy street in Ely with a fair amount of traffic. People driving home from work or going out to eat drive right past the final resting place of family and friends. You wonder how many people driving past at 40 mph give a sad nod to loved ones who are departed. And how many folks getting a new set of tires at the Big 8 ever wander across the road for a quick visit with the memories of those long gone. You see fresh flowers on some of the graves, sometimes on the graves of people who have been dead for 10, 20 years and more – colorful remembrances of lost relationships.

Ely was a mining town, populated with people from all over the world – Asians, Italians, Slavs, French Basques, English, Greeks, and Native Americans. It was a small-town reflection of American society at large, a melting pot of cultures, cuisines, and religions. It is a mix well-represented at the cemetery.

111

In a shady grove, set off to one side, is the section for Ely veterans who served their country. There you find the graves of veterans lined up in rank and file from World War I, World War II, Korea, Vietnam, and the newer ones from the current era. Ely's recognition of those who served.

Some of them have their wives buried next to them, joined in death as they were in life. There is even a father and a daughter – him a private from World War II, she a sergeant first class from the Vietnam War.

The Ely graveyard, like all graveyards, contains both mysteries and secrets. Who were the people interred beneath the sod? How did they die, and are their graves near their friends or beside their bitter enemies? And perhaps most of all, do the bones and withered flesh encased beneath the sod have any relation at all to the person who once was, or is it merely a remembrance for the ones left behind?

You may think such thoughts, but not for too long. The living must live. The dead are just one more reminder that we are all headed for the same place.

Life is short, joy is fleeting, and time is not to be wasted.

# Chapter 3: DYING WITH OUR BOOTS ON

**PREFACE:** We Americans work a lot. We babysit and mow lawns for extra money when we're kids. We work our way through school. We work a series of jobs, always pushing for promotions and to make more money. We work out at the gym. We spend weekends and vacations working around the house. We work on our relationships and to be good parents, children, friends and citizens. And then one day, we retire. For some of us, that's the end. Decades ago we read an article that said that pension plans were determined by the statistic that people who retire will die within three years of the day they left their jobs. Not so today. Some of us are living a few decades past the big party and gold watch. That's a lot of time to sit around enjoying our "well-deserved rest."

*Carmela*

# Essays

These Boots Are Made for Living      116

A New Day      118

I'm Back (Almost, Pretty Much, Sort Of)      121

My Pal, Jonathan Crockett Beaty      123

My Brawling Days Are Done, Or Are They?      127

Old Friends on a Long Journey      129

I've Turned into a Blooming Idiot      132

You Can't Go Home Again, But ...      133

My Other Little Brother, Ron Sherill      135

Five Things That Bug Me in My Old Age      137

Prison Blues      140

The Piano Came Home      151

The Man with the Bad Attitude      153

Why Are Experts Always So Wrong      155

Romance and Real Estate      157

# These Boots are Made for Living
### Carmela – June 13, 2020

My life with George has been a hoot. For more than 42 years, we've done pretty much everything together. We traveled and we stayed home. We loved and we fought and we played. We worked really, really hard. Sometimes, we worked so long and hard that there was little time for anything else. We paid a price for that, in terms of battered health and missed time with people we loved. But we also got a great benefit from it. We got a life.

Family and dear friends died. We battled health issues. We welcomed new babies and in-laws into the family. We delighted in nieces and nephews and Wonder Pets who came to live with us. We owned our own business – twice. We wrote books and thousands of essays. We worked for big corporations, non-profits, a university, and newspapers. At one point we were relegated to the "older generation" table at family weddings. We shared thousands of meals and drank thousands of lattes and margaritas with cherished friends, and we have seen each other's wrapping get a little more crinkly and a little more gray.

Through it all, we promised each other that we'd "die with our boots on."

That was all well and fine while we were stubbornly refusing to retire, but then one day, we did. After all those years of work, we just stopped. It was the right decision and one that George and I were both happy with. But I was apprehensive.

If we retired, how in Hell were we going to die with our boots on?

We jumped into retirement as we did everything else. We went face first. George, Henry and I emptied our home, got into the car, and drove around the country for a year.

Then we settled into a new home. For the first time in my life, I got enough sleep, could read as much as I wanted and had time to exercise – all things that caused me to wonder if I would ever really be tired again.

The thought that I might not exhaust myself on a daily basis worried me. I had always gauged my success in life by how many things I did each day, by how hard I worked, and by how tired I was each night.

But that's when I came to understand what it really means to die with my boots on. It doesn't mean I have to have a job working for somebody. I don't need to be paid for what I do. What it means, is that I have to continue to be part of the world. I need to do the things that matter to me. I started thinking about retirement as the time when I could do anything on earth that I want – maybe even everything I want.

The biggest lesson I've learned so far from retirement is that we humans should be outside more. Much, much more. We should spend almost all our time outside. I used to run from parking structure to parking structure, sometimes never setting foot outside in the course of a day. That was bad. Farmers work outside all day long. Our world is not structured that way, but maybe it should be.

These days – as I'm dying with my boots on, I walk for miles. I go to war with the preying manti who eat my caterpillars, and I know the name of every dog in the neighborhood. These are important things.

All it really takes to die with your boots on, is to never stop living, to never stop rushing face first into life. Maybe it's volunteering for a cause that you never dreamed you'd care about. Or taking up a sport or a hobby that you always thought was silly. Dying with your boots on doesn't mean having a job, it only means being smack dab in the middle of something – or a lot of things – that you love when you die. It doesn't get much better than that. So here I am – retired. Me, of all people.

But I've still got my boots on.

# A New Day

George – July 9, 2016

Writers as a group are a pathetic bunch of human beings. They are self-righteous and full of themselves one day; self-loathing and full of doubt the next. They plunge ahead, using words as weapons, flinging them wildly at those who have achieved success, wounding the innocent along with the guilty, then basking in the satisfaction that they have helped right some abstract and unstated wrong. They are self-indulgent, often irresponsible, full of preconceived notions and absolutely critical to the functioning of modern society in much the same way that rat poison is critical to the control of vermin. Writers, for the most part, don't write for the money. As a group, they are some of the least well-paid, skilled people in society. They do it for personal recognition. They do it in pursuit of influence. But mostly, they do it because they can't help themselves.

I should know. I am a writer.

In 1995, I was working at the Press-Telegram newspaper in Long Beach churning out stories assigned by editors, most of whom I did not respect. I was frustrated by the downward spiral of the newspaper business in general and by the desperate and often silly measures being taken by the people in charge to save something that was fatally flawed – the idea of a traditional newspaper.

It didn't take a rocket scientist to see that cable TV, the Internet, and the easy access to information had doomed the newspaper business, whether we loved it or not. And the people who paid the bills – the advertisers – were finding new places and ways to advertise that were both cheaper and more efficient than relying on newspapers.

But people in the newspaper business were in denial. What if we start putting salsa recipes on the Food Page in order to attract Hispanic readers? What if we print one page a week in Khmer to attract Cambodian readers? Let's close down the State Capitol bureau – politics is boring – and start doing frothy features about home and family.

None of which did anything at all to stop the decline.

Then a miracle happened. Not for the newspaper, it was already in its death throes, but for me. In their zeal to save their dying dinosaur, management at the Press-Telegram came up with a plan to reduce costs by reducing staff. They offered a "buy-out" to anybody who had worked there a prescribed number of years, was of a certain age, and who would agree to "retire."

I didn't have to think twice. I was delighted. Nobody had ever paid me to go away before, and I was not about to pass up that opportunity. I said thank you very much, took the money, and ran.

Not everybody did. Within a year, the paper was sold, the new owner slashed salaries 10 to 20 percent, and the people who were left either ate the loss of pay or hit the bricks to find new jobs.

When I left the paper in December of 1995, I had a plan. As a reporter, I had covered the Port of Long Beach and the Port of Los Angeles. It was a frustrating job, because the editors at the paper were not particularly interested in the business and money that flowed through the ports. No matter how hard I tried, I could not convince them that the ports were worthy of the same kind of coverage afforded local government and the surrounding communities.

Carmela Castorina, who wrote stories about ports and trade for the Pacific Shipper Magazine, agreed with me. What made it even more appealing was that Carmela and I were living together, and we were in love. We both wanted to publish a personal publication that reflected our point of view – which was that trade between nations is a good thing that benefits people on both sides of the deal.

But there was one thing that Carmela and I wanted to do first – get married. Although we had been together almost 20 years, we had never tied the knot. So, on December 16, 1995, Carmela Castorina became Carmela Cunningham, and I became the luckiest man on the planet. We had a two day honeymoon trip to Big Sur and then went straight to work trying to write enough copy to fill the beast we were birthing. We came up with 200 potential subscribers, who would get complimentary one-month subscriptions in order to entice them to sign up for a year, and we'd grow our subscriber list from there.

Since it was our personal publication, and by then we were both Cunninghams, we decided to call it The Cunningham Report.

So there in the wee hours of the first day of 1996, we composed our cover sheet note. We explained to our would-be readers who we were and what we were doing. We said we hoped they liked our new publication and said we were very excited to be joining an industry that had such potential to create prosperity and opportunity on a global scale.

Then we went home and collapsed. For the next six months, we worked every single day without break, feeding the monster that we had created, collecting new subscribers, attending every trade and transportation event in the state, and handing out business cards. On our first half-day off, we went out to lunch, and we didn't even talk about The Cunningham Report. We had a fight. Then we went home, got the first uninterrupted six-hour sleep we'd had in months, got up and went back to the office to start work on the next edition.

The next 15 years continued pretty much the same way. Producing The Cunningham Report was a huge high. It was our own business. We did it all the way we wanted. When the money came in, we put it into our bank account. Even better, when the kudos came in, they were all ours. Every artistic, creative, and business decision was ours. We loved it. But then one day, we decided we were through. We wanted to do something else. On December 13, 2010, we published the last Cunningham Report.

By mid-2011, we had launched our new business – the Reader Publishing Group. Publishing technology that had been developing for the previous few years provided the opportunity for small businesses to get into the publishing business – and that's what we did. At the same time that we were building the readerpublishing.com website and working with two other authors on their books, I wrote Kaboom, a gritty novel for people with short attention spans. I also wrote The Big Story, a novel about a crime reporter in the 1970s.

Then I got viral pericarditis – an infection around the heart that is cured by massive doses of anti-inflammatories and sleeping. And that's what I did – for a full year. Near the end of that year, the Port of Long Beach contacted Carmela and me about writing a history of the port. We went through another year of proposals and consideration and finally, by the middle of 2013, we began an 18-month project to somehow capture how that port – and to some extent, its sister port Los Angeles – came to be built and thrive. We were back to the 18-hour days and 7-day weeks that had marked The Cunningham Report years. Before the end of 2014, we had produced 500 hundred pages we dubbed Port Town. Then we got in the car and we drove. About 30,000 miles over the next year. We didn't live anywhere in particular. We weren't really going anywhere in particular, and besides some promotional appearances for Port Town, we didn't work much. We plotted our next move.

And then I had a stroke.

# I'm Back (Almost, Pretty Much, Sort Of)
## George – August 27, 2015

I'm not going to lie. Having a stroke, even a small one, is no walk in the park. It can shake you up, change the way you look at the world, and remind you that life does not go on forever. Life is finite. If there are things you want to accomplish, there are only so many years, so many months, and so many weeks, days, hours and minutes to accomplish them. This is true whether you are 7 years old or 70.

I suffered two relatively minor strokes late last month. I stupidly ignored the first one – there was no pain – and dismissed it as a case of being overly tired. The second one was impossible to ignore. At lunch at the Belmont Brewery in Long Beach, the conversation became disjointed, and although I could understand words and even phrases, I had no comprehension of what people were saying. I also had trouble seeing them. I did not tell anybody this information.

I have fought in a war, I have been in fist fights, I have lived by the male code – if you're not dead, shake it off and move on. I drove home, not my best decision considering my limited vision, and fell into bed. Within seconds, I was asleep and slept until the next morning.

When I awoke, I was still having vision problems, although I still did not tell anyone. Finally, Carmela nagged that information out of me. Unburdened by male pride and stubbornness, Carmela rushed me to Kaiser for an emergency eye exam, where they discovered I have glaucoma. They also discovered I had limited to no vision in the upper right quadrant of both eyes. That is not an eye problem – that is a brain problem.

By that evening, I was lying in a hospital room in one of those little backless gowns with an IV in my arm and peeing into a little plastic container that Carmela held for me.

When I was in Vietnam, Carmela was 9 years old. Too bad. We could have used somebody like her when the bullets started flying. This whole experience was much worse for her than for me, but she did not once fall apart, at least not until it was all over.

Fortunately for me, my stroke turned out to be a minor one – a reminder from the gods about what's important and what is not. Having seen the effect it had Carmela – I cannot, and will not – call it a blessing, but you take from such experiences the things that are important and positive and accept the things that are not as part of the price you pay.

So now, I'm back. Not quite as strong as I was, but a lot smarter. After a scheduled CAT scan showed that any remaining blood clots in my brain are gone, I was put on warfarin – the generic name for Coumadin – a blood thinner that hopefully will prevent a repeat experience.

Next week I will go back to the doctor to have my eyes checked, to see if I have regained peripheral vision. I am sure that I have. I find myself checking it all the time as Carmela maneuvers through traffic. At first I thought maybe my peripheral vision was returning as the doctors said it might. But then I worried it was just the result of wishful thinking. Now I am sure of it. The doctors will be checking it out next week and maybe, just maybe, I will be able to drive again. I hope so. Carmela, who hates to drive, hopes so, and so does Henry, who likes to curl up on Carmela's lap while I drive.

Lessons learned and promises and advice to my friends – and even to my enemies:

*As my pal, Freddy Nietzsche once said, anything that doesn't kill you, makes you stronger.*

*Everybody from birth on, has a finite number of days on the planet. Identify what is important to you, learn from your mistakes, and try to take some joy in each and every day you have.*

*Take care of yourself. If you experience any confusion or other such symptoms, go immediately to the emergency room and tell them you think you may have had a stroke. There is a four-hour window in which they can mitigate the damage.*

*Unless I regain full vision, I will not drive. Your children are safe from me.*

*This final promise is to my loyal and loving wife. I plan to live forever. I go into this battle understanding that I will most certainly lose. But when that time does come, I plan to go down fighting.*

# My Pal, Jonathan Crockett Beaty

George – July 7, 2020

When I talk about Jonathan Crockett Beaty being an old friend, I not only mean that I have known him a long time – longer than any living friend I have – but also that like me, he is old. Jonathan has spent his life railing against the darkness. He is stubbornly opposed to fitting in, to being content with life as assigned to him, and to being ordinary.

That may be the only thing the two of us have in common. Although we tend to respectfully disagree on much of the rest of the world in which we live, a long talk with Jonathan is worth at least two years of higher education and is easily twice as interesting.

I first met Jonathan in 1969, when I joined the staff at the Daily Breeze newspaper in Torrance, California. I was 29, he was 32.

Jonathan never graduated from college or took courses in journalism, which was one of the reasons he was so good at being one. I had recently gotten a degree in journalism from the University of Florida.

Journalism is one of those degrees that is easy to get. I had been an engineering student before I decided – after an extended absence from the university, which included three years in the Army and almost a year working on a construction project in Puerto Rico – that I wanted to switch majors.

Luckily, I got my degree at an advanced age – graduating at 28

– which meant I had quite a bit of life experience before going back to school. I had reached an age of discerning academic BS from truth.

Jonathan also had the kind of experience you don't get at a university. He had worked various jobs, including at an aerospace company and a gig with a power company in the piney wilderness of British Columbia. He had left there after his second wife wanted to move back to Wilmington, California – a low-rent neighborhood north of the Los Angeles harbor area.

He started his own business, a janitorial service cleaning offices at night, before looking around for something more interesting. He decided on journalism and got a job at the Daily Breeze shortly before I had.

I liked Jonathan as soon as I met him. He had a sort of swagger about him that was compelling. He had used his press credential to finagle a concealed carry permit from a local police department. Tucked in a shoulder holster beneath his sports coat he was packing a 1911 Colt .45 automatic pistol – the same model of pistol I had carried during my tour in Vietnam.

At the time, I owned a 21-foot sailboat named the Harvey Wallbanger – after the cocktail of the same name. I moored the Harvey Wallbanger at the Redondo Beach Marina, and one day I invited Jonathan out for a sail. We went out on a choppy sea, bobbing around, drinking beer and throwing the cans in the ocean. After a while, Jonathan pulled out his .45 and began shooting at the cans as they floated away on the waves.

The .45 was a good close-in weapon with a big slow-moving bullet that was deadly and great for close-in combat, but not at all accurate at any kind of distance. After firing a few rounds, Jonathan handed over his pistol for me to try. We threw an empty into the ocean, and I took aim and squeezed off a shot – sending the can flying.

It was totally a lucky shot, but Jonathan was amazed.

"Here, do it again," he said.

I refused, like I didn't want to show off. But from that day on, we were buddies.

Jonathan was a relentless reporter, a shameless self-promoter, a champion bull-shitter, and a kind man to his friends. I was lucky enough to be among that group.

There is not enough time or space to recount all the stories and adventures with Jonathan, but a few stand out like old photos burned imperfectly into my memory.

Jonathan was a free-range dad as most fathers our age were at the time.

He had two daughters, Jamaica and Jordann from his first

marriage. I remember a long ride north on Pacific Coast Highway, back when the girls were in their pre-teens, and they taught me the all the words to the McDonald's jingle:

*"Two all-beef patties*
*Special sauce, lettuce, cheese*
*Pickles, onions on a sesame seed bun"*

But they had memorized it backwards as in:

*"Bun, seed, sesame, a onions pickles ..."*

We sang it for at least 100 miles, each time them chastising me when I got it wrong.

It was a happy memory, with a sad ending. Jordann died a few years later in a fall off an upper floor balcony.

Jonathan also had a son, "Little Jonathan," by his second wife. I skipped out of work at the Orange County Register one afternoon in the late 70s for lunch with Jonathan and Little Jonathan, and we ended up, after several hours of drinking, taking off for Ensenada, Mexico. Jonathan and I proceeded to continue drinking at Hussong's Cantina while Little Jonathan made friends with the street kids outside.

I missed Jonathan's marriage to his third wife Linda, and I still regret it.

As with everything in Jonathan's life, it was done with style. Jonathan had talked a local Toyota dealer in Manhattan Beach into giving him a Toyota Land Cruiser for an "expedition" to Central America. To launch the expedition, Jonathan talked the Port of Los Angeles – which he covered as a reporter – into hosting the wedding onboard the port's yacht. He sent out invitations to all the press and TV stations.

This was the same day I decided to buy a motorcycle, which I had planned to ride to the wedding. I had never driven a motorcycle before, but I was full of confidence and bravado. The first thing I wanted to do was pop a wheelie and get that machine up on its back wheel. How hard could it be? It turned out to be harder than one might think.

I ended up bloody and bruised and missing the wedding ceremony.

As it turned out, Jonathan and Linda split for Central America, had lots of adventures, met a multitude of important political leaders, explored ancient ruins, and came home with a load of prime dope hidden in a sealed plastic tube in their gas tank.

Before they crossed the border, he and Linda adopted a

respectable attitude of law-abiding citizens, slapped a "Support Your Local Police" sticker on the bumper, and passed through customs like a breeze.

It was never that Jonathan was amoral. He has always had his own moral code, which according to circumstance may or may not have coincided with what society demanded.

Over the years things changed, and Jonathan and I went our separate ways for a while. I went through a bit of a tough time in my life, where I temporarily lost my way and lost some of the friendship that was once so important to me. I also gave up the kind of heavy drinking Jonathan and I used to do. After I met and married Carmela, I found myself less compelled by the sharp taste of whisky on my tongue as a daily habit.

Jonathan ended up at Time magazine, where he traveled the world, interviewed drug lords in their home lairs, investigated crooked financial dealings, hobnobbed with celebrities, and appeared on the nightly network news shows to talk about the issues of the day. He and fellow Time correspondent S.C. Gwynne wrote "The Outlaw Bank: A Wild Ride into the Secret Heart of BCCI." The 1993 book exposed the operations of the Bank of Credit and Commerce International, a financial institution that helped move money for terrorists, criminals and corrupt governments worldwide.

Today, Jonathan lives on a hilltop in New Mexico, miles from the nearest paved road. He is in his 80s, still drinking whisky, smoking dope, and shooting guns. He has battled cancer, heart disease, snake bite, and scrapes with the law. Against all odds, he is still alive.

And against all odds, so am I.

# My Brawling Days Are Done, or Are They?

### George – May 5, 2017

You get old, and you get mellow, and after a while, you start thinking like an old man, which is exactly who you are. You become a kinder person, you overlook people's flaws, and you start mistaking that for wisdom. When you look back at your younger days, you begin to think what a jerk "that guy" was.

So you move to a 55-and up retirement community for "active seniors" and you settle in. Then one day, you and your wife go to breakfast at the Sandwedge, which is the cutesy name for the little coffee shop at the golf course. And while you are eating your bacon and eggs and drinking your coffee, you see an old guy with a dead snake, going over to a table where four old ladies are chatting among themselves. The old man interrupts their conversation, brandishes the snake, thrusting it toward them to give them a scare. They recoil and give him that pained smile that women get when they are pretending to be nice.

"I hope he doesn't come over here with that stupid thing," Carmela says, and I assure her that he won't. So, we continue our conversation about this and that, and right in the middle of our talk, the old man comes over, interrupts us, and thrusts the snake – which turns out to be a realistic looking fake – in Carmela's face.

"Please don't do that," she says in a calm but curt tone. But he just laughs and does it again. And that's when all my old-man kindness and wisdom fly out the window.

"Get the f*** away from us," I tell him loudly. The problem is, I say it so loudly, that all the folks in the restaurant stop eating and stare at us, including the old man with the snake, who looks confused.

"Get the f*** out of here," I tell him again as I jump up out of my seat, knocking my chair over in the process.

At this point the other old guy flees out the door.

It would seem like mission accomplished, but to tell you the truth, I immediately felt ashamed. I try very hard to be tolerant, but I scared an old man – no matter how obnoxious he may have been. I used bad language – I don't talk like that anymore. And I made a scene and interrupted everybody's breakfast by picking on a senior citizen.

But when I got home, I looked in the mirror and once again rediscovered the awful truth. I'm a senior citizen too. The old man and I are probably about the same age. He didn't have to run out the door. He could have stood his ground and told me to go f*** myself. Then we could have thrown some punches, maybe wrestled around on the floor, and gotten busted by the Sun Lakes security team.

Who knows, after it was all over, the old man and I might have had a beer and ended up being friends.

Stranger things have happened.

# Old Friends on a Long Journey

George – November 11, 2021

I'm not much for annual celebrations, but I became part of one a few years back which we called the "Old Pals Brunch." The nucleus of it were my long-time pals Larry "Lash" LaRue, Susan Pack and me. We'd get together on New Year's Day for brunch. We went to restaurants a few times, but early on it moved to my home. No matter how little we friends had seen or heard from each other through the old year, we always got together at the beginning of the new year. We would eat and laugh and talk about the old days and all our plans for the days to come. Our mates Patrick, Marie and Carmela – were part of it of course. But they were late-comers to our friendship.

It was a wonderful celebration which quickly became a tradition that Carmela and I looked forward to each year. Then Larry died in 2017, and although we still try to get together with Susan and her husband Patrick every January 1, life intervenes – illnesses, injuries, and of course the dreaded Covid lockdown that kept close friends and family apart.

Carmela and I had lunch with Susan and Patrick last week, and we talked and laughed so much that it was surprising to think we hadn't seen each other in more than two years.

Susan and Larry were friends long before I came on the scene. They were journalism students at Cal State Long Beach in the early 1970s. After college, Lash went off to Nebraska to become a reporter at the Omaha World Herald. Susan got a job at the Orange County Register.

I moved to California in 1969, after graduating from the University of Florida, despite warnings from folks I knew, cautioning me not to go. People are crazy out there, they said. What they failed to consider was that I was crazy too.

So, I packed up my bags and moved to California and got a job at the South Bay Daily Breeze in Torrance. After a couple of years at the Daily Breeze, and another couple of lost years trying to figure out what I wanted to do next, I ended up at City News Service, a wire service in downtown Los Angeles. I went from there to publishing a weekly mobile home newspaper, before giving it up and applying for a job at the Register in Orange County – about the same time as Lash was joining the staff there.

And that's where I met Susan. The three of us didn't exactly hang out together, but we enjoyed a kind of happy and close friendship, one in which we looked out for one another. At some point Susan left the Register for greener pastures, working in public relations at Rockwell International.

After Lash quit his job at the Register and worked as a private investigator for a while, he finally landed a job at the Long Beach Press Telegram. When a couple of jobs opened up there, he put in a good word for Susan and me. We both applied and were both hired.

Later, Susan tipped off my then-girlfriend, now-wife Carmela Castorina about an opening at Rockwell. Carmela applied, got the job doing public relations for the B1 bomber project, working as editor of the company newsletter and writing about everybody from workers on the assembly line to test pilots at Edwards Air Force Base.

At one point, Susan quit her job at the Press-Telegram for a new gig at the Register Guard in Eugene, Oregon. For old-guard journalists – back in the day when journalism was fun – part of the draw was gathering after work in smoke-filled taverns like the Press Club bar across the street from the Press-Telegram and rehashing their days and their stories.

The Register Guard was not like that. There was no reporter hangout. After work, writers went home to their families. Instead of drinking the night away, they spent their off-duty time at little league games and being moms and dads. Susan missed the old-school ways and wanted to come back to Long Beach.

I lobbied for her, cornering the managing editor as he was using the urinal in the men's room, to make the case for hiring Susan back. I'm not claiming I tipped the balance in her favor – she was a good writer and made a strong case for herself – but I had her back as she had always had mine.

Unfortunately, journalism stopped being fun when a new generation of earnest, politically correct reporters and editors came on the scene. Local newspapers were dying. I married Carmela and we started our own newsletter on West Coast ports.

The Press-Telegram was sold off to a company more interested in cashing out the physical assets than daily journalism, and the best members of the staff found other occupations. Susan ended up working PR for Toyota. By then, Lash was covering baseball at the Tacoma News Tribune. He was a popular sports writer there for years until he was finally taken off the beat as the financially strapped Tribune scaled back its sports coverage. He wrote a column for a few years, before he finally retired.

None of us were ever perfect people or even responsible, and we were surely not boring pillars of the community. Thank God for that! We all had our ups and downs – divorces, heart breaks, happy times, unhappy times, and our own personal track records of triumphs and tragedies.

But we all ended up with people we loved and lives lived on our own terms.

Lash is gone now, and Susan and I are both getting old. We're living the life we were meant to live with the people we were meant to live it with and basking in the warmth of each and every day.

I like to think we've still got each other's backs.

# I've Turned into a Blooming Idiot

George – May 7, 2019

Maybe it's just my age or maybe it's the political and social times in which I live, but the older I get, the more I find myself disliking people and politics and the more I am drawn to dogs and flowers.

We humans have lived through the Socratic Age, the Romance Age, the Medieval Age, the Renaissance, the Age of Reason, the Age of Enlightenment, and the Modern Age. Throughout history, people looked at the world and tried to understand it and figure out where we all fit into the scheme of things.

Here's the truth.

We are currently living in the Age of Stupidity. It's an age where people stake out a political or social position and only talk to people who agree precisely in whatever dogma they happen to favor. And the more they talk to people who are in complete agreement with themselves, the more convinced they become that they are the enlightened ones and that people who disagree with them are a bunch of ignoramuses, or in the words of one politician, deplorables.

I have decided to start my own age – The Age of Dogs, Flowers and Good Food. The roses are in bloom. The pups are enjoying the warmer weather. And Carmela has a big pot of jambalaya simmering in the kitchen.

The Age of Dogs, Flowers and Good Food may not go down in history as a major movement, but that's OK.

It's a nice place to spend some time.

# You Can't Go Home Again, But ...
## George – August 30, 2017

Thomas Wolfe famously said "You can't go home again." And he was right. You can't go home again because home has changed, the people have changed, the places have changed and you have changed as well. Home is not the same place you left, and you are not the same person who left there.

But you can go back to a place where you once lived, and conjure up the people who were once part of your life there and of the child you once were and who once was part of the place and the community.

I was conjuring big time last week during a visit to my home town of St. Petersburg, Florida. There was a time, right after World War II, when I was just a little kid, and my mother and father were still in their 20s, and they were young and happy and looking forward to making more babies and getting on with their lives.

It was different being a kid back then, and I had learned the rules early on: Children were made to be seen, not heard.

That meant you could stick around and watch and listen, but you couldn't interrupt the grownups and when you were addressed, you said "yes sir" or "yes ma'am," and you never, ever talked back unless you wanted your fanny slapped. It wasn't a bad system because when you listened to adults, you learned about being an adult and about the world outside your immediate family.

My dad's younger brother, Henry Cunningham was also back from the war. He had married my Aunt May, and they lived down the street. The four of them would go out dancing together, and I would get to listen to their stories when they came home. One of their places was the Gulfport Casino. It wasn't a gambling casino, but rather, it was a casino in the original sense, a sort of community center, where people could get together to socialize and hold special events. Every week, there would be dances at the Casino and sometimes my parents and my uncle and aunt would go there to dance.

Gulfport at the time was a little working-class community with a population of fishermen, boatwrights, carpenters, painters, mechanics and other blue-collar folks. Good people, but generally not very sophisticated. My parents and my aunt and uncle would come home after these dances and laugh about what they called the "Gulfport Pump Handle." They would dance around, with one arm around the other's waist and the opposite arms extended straight out, hands joined, pumping up and down to the music.

Then they would laugh, and I would laugh too, although I had never been to a dance and had no idea how you were supposed to do it. As a matter of fact, I still don't.

Those were happy years for my mother and father and for my aunt and uncle, and as the oldest of my generation I was soaking it all in. I would listen and learn, and think about how I would act when I became a grownup – although at that stage of life, being an adult seemed so far in the future that it was more a concept than a reality. Kind of like going to heaven or getting on a spaceship and flying to the moon.

My mom and my aunt were both full of life and happy to be out in the world with their husbands. It was a nice time for them and for me, but such times always end. My mother and father separated some years later, and he died of pancreatic cancer in 1965. My Uncle Henry died in 1986, my mother in 2001, and my Aunt May in 2013.

Thomas Wolfe was correct. You really can't go home again. But you can take a moment to stop and remember what once was and what will never be again.

It's a sweet thing to do on a sunny afternoon in Gulfport, Florida, but it's a sad thing as well.

# My Other Little Brother, Ron Sherill
## George – August 27, 2020

My mother had three sons, but if you look at old pictures there is often a fourth young man included in the Cunningham group of brothers. That young man is Ron Sherill. Ron has been part of the clan – at times close, at other times less so – since he was a teenager.

Ron was there when my brother Chuck was killed in a workplace accident in 1971. It happened right in front of him, and I remember Ron curled up on the couch in our ramshackle home, distraught and hurting after I flew back home to bury my little brother. He traveled with my other brother Bill, when they were both young and adventurous, careening across the country, living on credit cards they had no intention of paying back, bumming rides and hopping trains. He was with Bill when Bill was pushing barges at the helm of a tug, running supplies to the oil islands off the Texas coast.

And now, as a co-survivor of the last of the three Cunningham brothers, he is part of my life as well.

Ron is a walking miracle. He was supposed to die of advanced cancer several years back when doctors gave him only months to live. He celebrated Christmas early that year because nobody expected him to be around for the actual holiday itself. There have been many happy Christmases since then, and my unofficial brother Ron is still here, still hanging around, enjoying life, and appreciating every day he spends above the ground rather than planted below it.

Ron is an artist, a lover of animals, and an admirer of beautiful things. I have one of his pictures hanging in my office. I see it every time I sit down to work, so every day I think of him.

Ron is old now, his once youthful zest and energy only slightly diminished by age and illness. But every happy day is a miracle for Ron and an inspiration for his unofficial older brother.

That would be me.

# Five Things that Bug Me in My Old Age

George – August 6, 2019

As I get old, I have discovered two things.

One, things that used to drive me crazy, no longer do. You know, live and let live. You don't have to agree with me. Why would I care if you do or you don't?

And two, some things that used to be just annoying, now tend to drive me nuts. I don't pretend it makes any sense. In fact it doesn't make any sense. It just is what it is.

For instance:

## ONE: People I Don't Know Calling Me by My First Name

I go to the bank, or I go to a hotel, or I go to anywhere else where I have to show an ID, and whomever I am dealing with thinks that if they call me by my first name I'll feel like they are my friends. This is particularly galling when my wanna-be new pal is about 20 years old.

You're probably thinking how petty of me, and you're probably right. But I grew up in the South, where you addressed everybody older than you as "Sir" or "Ma'am." Even if you were 40 and they were 60, you still showed them the respect that comes with age.

This also bugs me with cops who pull me over on the freeway. Here's some kid that just got out of high school five years ago, saying:

"Well, George, do you know how fast you were driving?" I know exactly how fast I was going, but I play it dumb.

"No officer, I'm afraid I don't," I say.

I am not about to squeal on myself.

Now I don't fault the officer for stopping me for speeding, that's the job. But unless he wants me to call him Bobby or Randy or Susie, he really needs to address me as Mr. Cunningham.

So, I usually come off as an old guy with a bad attitude. That's OK. I can live with that.

## TWO: People Who Drive Slow in the Car Pool Lane

Let's get one thing straight right off. There is the law as it is written down in the vehicle code and there's the real-world law

137

that regular people follow. One of those real-world laws is that nobody drives at the speed limit in the car pool lane unless traffic is really jammed up.

But every once in a while, you get stuck behind some jerk who's driving at 55 or 60 in the car pool lane, with a wide-open lane in front of him and all the drivers to the right zooming by at 75 and 80 mph. I mean this is California, man. Everybody speeds, and we all drive too close together. That's the only way the freeways work.

Once some timid jerk starts hitting the brakes, the whole system breaks down into a stop-and-go nightmare.

## THREE: Overly Friendly Cashiers or Customers Who Hold Up the Line

I may be a grumpy old man, but there's a time and a place for everything. I hate waiting in line at the supermarket with my ice cream getting softer by the minute while some person – I don't want to be sexist, but it's usually a woman – takes her own sweet time to check out.

And it's not just her. Sometimes the cashier is just as bad.

"That will be $96.43," the cashier will say and the customer will start digging in her purse to pay the bill. I don't want to be insensitive, but she had to know that there would come this moment when money would have to change hands. So, she reaches down in slow motion, opens up her purse, takes out her checkbook and starts writing a check. I mean for Heaven's sake, who the Hell buys things with checks anymore?

Then the cashier will see that the customer has a picture in her wallet of her grandchild or her dog or a day at the beach, and the clerk feels the need to comment on it. And, while my ice cream is slipping from solid to liquid, the two of them ramble on.

"Isn't that adorable," the cashier might say, and the customer will stop writing her check to tell her how her child or her dog is smart as a whip.

Finally, I very politely say, "Isn't that nice, but could you please just pay your bill, take your groceries and go home, so I can get home and put my ice cream in the freezer?"

And all of a sudden, I'm the bad guy. Go figure.

## FOUR: Phone Mail and Being Put on Hold

I am old enough to remember when you called some company and a person answered the phone. It was a custom that worked pretty well. Now a robot answers the phone and gives you a list of options: What language do you want to use, Press One for English, Two for Spanish, Three for Khmer, Four for Chinese, etc., etc., etc.

Then the phone mail Hell tries to figure out what you want to talk about. Another list of options, which most often does not include anything that I want. So I pick the one that seems the closest, and I wait, listening to on-hold tunes such as "Satisfaction" by the 101 Living Strings orchestra, as the minutes go by and death gets closer with each tick of the clock.

And the real message is this: Your time is not valuable to us. We don't really give a darn what your problem is. And maybe if we draw this out long enough you will give up and just go away. And sometimes I do ... forever.

## FIVE: Surveys and Polls

Another bunch of people who think my time is not valuable are pollsters and survey-takers. The first ones want to ask me a series of questions about who I'm going to vote for and the second ones are customer service folks who want to know how happy or unhappy I was with something they had sold me.

The first group is dismissed out of hand. It's none of their business for whom I plan to vote, or what I may think about the state of the world. They're getting paid to ask me the questions, but they don't plan to pay me to answer them. I suspect I end up in the undecided category or maybe they pretend they couldn't get ahold of me, so my opinion isn't counted.

The second group is presumably asking questions so they can improve their service by finding out what their company is doing right and what it is doing wrong. But here's the problem. I don't mind answering two or three or even four questions about my experience with their company, but that's never enough.

These surveys are drawn up by a committee somewhere and everybody on that committee has a slightly different idea of what questions to ask and how to ask them. So I end up with 20 minutes of questions many of which are redundant and lots of which don't apply.

I don't want to be an old grump or anything. But clearly I am.

# Prison Blues

Carmela - April 13, 2020

A couple years after I retired, I decided to do volunteer work with women who were in prison, helping them find their ways back into society after they had served their time and were released back into the free world. I'm a firm believer in good, hard, earn-your-own-way work. I believe work makes you free. And I believe that getting jobs is the best chance these women had to make a life for themselves after prison.

So, how does a person who's in prison find her way to a job?

My spiel to the women was this. You have to respect yourself – otherwise no one else will. You have to have a great attitude. You have to tell the truth. You have to be willing to work hard. You have to see yourself as that good person who is willing to work hard, and you have to sell that vision to potential employers. We identified what jobs women might apply for when they were released, and worked on creating solid resumes and cover letters, good interview skills, and dressing well for interviews.

We also talked about how to answer the tough questions – most specifically, "so what have you been doing for the past two years?" I shouldn't have been surprised when the first response from every woman was to shout out a lie.

"I was taking care of my sick grandmother," was a favorite.

*\*\*\**

The rules for volunteering at a prison are strict.

I was not to bring a phone, pens, jewelry, purse or any other personal item into the prison. I could not wear open-toed shoes. I was not to tell people anything at all about myself or family, turn my back on prisoners, or let anyone touch me or be within two feet of me. I was not to allow anyone to get behind me or between me and the locked, thick metal door that led out of the unit.

I also had to sign a waiver saying that I understood that if I was taken hostage, the prison would not negotiate for my release. This was all fine with me. I was excited to begin.

For the next nine months, I met with prisoners one day every week. Some days stood out more than others.

## May 28, 2018 – Day One

I went to the prison ready to help people. I knew I wasn't going to walk in like Mary Poppins visiting the Banks children for the first time. That was probably my only correct assumption.

The women were not eagerly awaiting my arrival or happy to see me. Some of them were mad I had come because it meant the common TV had to be turned off. Some begrudgingly agreed to participate in my workshop because if they finished the material and passed a test, it would make them eligible for a week's time off their sentences. Some were bored to death and figured that sitting up talking to someone new was better than lying in bed staring at the ceiling. And others just wanted the stubby little pencil that they got to keep at the end of the class.

I saw and heard a lot of things on that first day that I had not expected.

One thing I did not expect was how the deputies reacted to the program I was participating in. Some were disinterested as to why I was there or what I was attempting to do. Some thought I was truly wasting my time – and theirs. One explained that her job was to keep prisoners safe while they were there. What happened when they got out was not her – or the Sheriff's concern. The prison system was not funded to deal with prisoners when they were released, she said. The prison's funding was for incarceration. What prisoners did when they got out was someone else's job – someone else's problem.

Fair enough.

In the prison where I worked, there were 22 pods for women. Each pod had four housing units. A female deputy sat up in a high, bullet-proof booth that was in the middle of each pod, with the housing units around it. The deputy had a closed circuit TV that spied into each unit in turn, and she could also look through the bullet-proof glass into each unit. There were heavy metal locked doors leading into each unit, each with a slot through which prisoners could slip notes - or "kites" - to deputies to pass on to prison officials. The door locks were electronically controlled by the deputy who sat up in the middle booth.

It was raining hard on my first day at the prison. I walked to an outside booth and showed my ID badge, which allowed me into the prison and to wander on my own through most areas. The guard at the booth instructed me to the first gate. I pushed the buzzer, held my badge up to the sky and waited for the door to open. When it did, I said, "thank you" into the rain and walked through. I repeated that exercise nine more times before I got to the pod I was assigned to. On the way, I traveled through an outside chain-link-enclosed dirt pathway. Twice, groups of male inmates, attended by a couple deputies, were being marched through, and I had to go to the nearest locked gate, buzz and show

141

my badge so the gate would open and I could exit the walkway until the prisoners and deputies passed. I had to buzz and show my badge again to get back into the walkway.

When I got to my assigned pod, I explained to the deputy who I was and why I was there. She told me the rules.

Prisoners had to be sitting at my table or lying down in their beds when I was in the cell. No one was allowed behind me – ever. No one could touch me. I couldn't give anyone anything besides a study guide and a short, stubby pencil. I couldn't give anyone two pencils – held together with sharp points jutting outward, the pencils could be made into a stabbing weapon. I couldn't take anything from any of the women – not even a scrap of paper. No one could use the toilet without my permission. No one could leave the table or bed without my permission. I should buzz the deputy in the middle booth when I wanted to leave.

In each housing unit, there are ten bunk beds, five lining each side of the room. There is a long steel table bolted to the floor in the middle of the room, ten bolted-down stools line each side of the table. There is a bolted-down TV high up and across from the one door into the cell.

The TV is almost always on in the cell, unless the deputy turns it off – for whatever reason she chooses, or for no reason at all. When I visited, she would turn off the TV, no matter who was watching it, and no matter what part of the program was on.

There are two toilets at the end of each housing unit that sit about ten feet from each other. They are directly across from where I sat with my back to the door. The toilets are both behind cinder block walls that are less than four feet high. When women sit on the toilets, I can see their heads and shoulders. When they stand up to wipe, I can see the motions.

The first time I entered a housing unit, the humidity was oppressive. That's because there are two glassed-in showers at the end of the room, near the toilets. They are behind the waist-high cinder-block walls, under the TV. When the women shower, the entire housing unit steams up.

Each woman keeps all of her belongings in a box about 20 x 20 x 8 inches, with her booking number on the outside. The boxes hold all sorts of things. Drawings from their kids. A couple slices of wheat bread. A banana. Stapled-together pieces of paper, a paperback book. Photos. Juice boxes. Lip gloss. Nothing sharp. Nothing dangerous. Nothing that could be made dangerous. Some women decorate their boxes.

That first day, I sat down to a group of ten women. The group didn't look scary or mean or like criminals. I did not know why they were in jail or how long they would be there. I would never find out that information.

A surprising number of inmates came from nursing and childcare careers. LVNs, nursing assistants, medical assistants, home care workers, day care owners. I wondered what landed so many people from those careers in prison. Many of them thought that they'd go back to the same jobs. Would they? Could they?

Most of the women were personable, funny, caring people. But as my two-hour workshop went on, I noticed things. Even though they are adults, the prisoners would push like children do. If one asked to go to the bathroom, and I said yes, all of them wanted to go. They *had* to go. They had to go *sooooo* bad. It was absurd that I was supposed to decide whether these grown women could go to the bathroom, but that's the rule. When I was in the unit, I was in charge of their movements. I was in charge of when they peed.

I felt uncomfortable with the rules – the prisoners are all adults. Why did I have "say" over them?

I have always thought that the worst job ever would be that of a prison guard. I've always hated the thought of it. I think it brutalizes and diminishes the guards as much as the prisoners. I unwittingly became a pseudo-guard when I started doing this volunteer work. Part of my job was to keep order while I was in the housing unit. I didn't like it.

\*\*\*

Early on, I knew that I didn't like going to the prison. I didn't understand why at first, but I started getting in a bad mood about 48 hours prior to my visits. I generally liked working with the women, but I hated going to the prison. Prison gates and solid heavy doors clanged shut behind me everywhere I went. I had to buzz to get through those gates and doors, and that disembodied pair of eyes that was always watching me on camera never did bother to respond when I said "thank you" up into the sky. That depressed me. Prison is depressing.

I would never find out what happened to any of the women I worked with. I spent far too many hours fretting about who would get out and get jobs and support themselves and their families, and wondering who would get out and into more trouble, and be right back where I had found them in the first place.

## August 9, 2018

I didn't do very well in prison this day. My presentation was good. The women were engaged, and I think the enthusiasm and motivation were valuable.

But then, I let one inmate shake my hand. How could I not? I keep talking to them about self-respect. I tell them to look people in the eye. To stand up straight. To smile. To shake peoples' hands. How could I not give this woman mine when she reached for it? But it was stupid. It set the tone for the day. The tone was that I was willing to let them break a rule. And if I'd let them slide on one rule – maybe they could break others as well.

I gave one heavily pregnant woman permission to get up and use the toilet. Pregnant women need to use the toilet a lot. When others immediately asked, I said it was fine for them to go too. I let them go to their bunks and get things. I let them get up and get cups of water. All things they were not supposed to do when I was in the cell.

Prisoners participating in the program were supposed to sit at their bolted-to-the-floor stools and not get up until I left the unit. Prisoners not participating were supposed to stay on their bunks until I left the unit. But it seemed somehow disrespectful and rude for me to tell grown women to stay in their seats and stay in their bunks. That means I didn't enforce the rules, I didn't maintain order as I was supposed to. Letting the prisoners move about the housing unit to that extent led to two of them – at separate times - walking behind me – a safety violation that is absolutely never allowed.

I felt uncomfortable each time one of the prisoners was behind me. I didn't feel threatened, but I was aware that the potential was high for a problem that could endanger me or cause a situation that would require armed deputies to come into the unit. If an inmate had made an untoward move toward me, it could have escalated into a situation in which people were hurt.

That was not acceptable.

The interesting moment came when another inmate chastised one of the women behind me.

"Go to the other end of the table. You know you are not supposed to be behind her."

The inmate who had been standing behind me said, "oh, I'm sorry" and moved away, but it was clear she was just pushing limits. That's what people who are incarcerated do. They push limits. As a Class I level volunteer who was allowed to go into housing units of 20 women, part of my job was to make sure people did not push the limits while I was there.

That day, when I left the unit and went walking through the yard, there was a large male deputy talking with a female prisoner. I did not feel at all threatened. But, when I got within about five yards of them, the deputy said to the woman, "turn around and face the wall." She did so without hesitation.

It creeped me out. I hated it. It seemed so wrong. I was not afraid of her. I didn't see that she could cause any trouble. But the deputy was following the rules. He was maintaining order.

I have no problem giving adults direction and ensuring that they follow it. The problem is that prisoners tend not to act like adults, and so they can't be treated in the usual way we treat other adults. Even though I was a volunteer "teacher" and not a "jailer," it was incumbent on me to keep order.

Volunteering at the prison put me in a situation where approving reasonable requests and polite behavior were met with people pushing limits and breaking rules. Prisoners are required to live by these rules because they have committed crimes and are being punished for it. When people go to prison, they lose many of their rights. They lose their freedom. They lose their privacy. They lose the right to quiet. They lose most of their right to make their own choices.

Working with prisoners was a new challenge for me – and I was not altogether sure I could meet it. If I didn't learn how to maintain order and enforce rules in a very clear, direct, vocal way, I couldn't help them. If I couldn't make myself act in a way that seemed pretty disrespectful to me – I couldn't do my job.

I knew that working in the prison, doing something I believe is hugely important, would change me.

I just had to figure out how much.

## September 13, 2018

I went into the prison feeling pretty good. The previous week was great, and I hoped for the same this day. In my last visit, we had gotten a good discussion going about dignity and self-respect. Everyone was engaged. Several of the women had really interesting jobs before they were in prison – including two who didn't speak English. Through others who were bi-lingual, I learned that one was a "quincenara event planner." She made beautiful cakes and dresses for these important occasions. The other was a political campaigner and aide for politicians in Mexico. Think Kellyanne Conway with black hair and a Mexican accent.

One woman wanted to be a farmer when she left prison, one wanted to be an auto mechanic and two wanted to be casino owners. Not dealers. Owners.

The conversation had gotten people talking about where to get training and produced offers of networking help. Things couldn't have gone better. Was I ever feeling pleased with myself when I left the prison that previous week.

But that was absolutely not how things went the following week. This new day, everything was horrible.

There were only four women signed up, and another woman added her name to the list when I came in, making a total of five.

Before I could introduce myself or explain how the day would go, one of the women started talking. She said that she didn't really need this class and that any idiot knew what was in the class. She said she was only doing the program so she'd be eligible for the week's credit she could earn and that she wanted to take the test right then.

I told her that the week's credit was based on participating in the class and *then* taking the test. She continued to demand to take the test right then and to say that she didn't need the class because she could "get any job she wanted, whenever she wanted."

One thing I had already learned, is that housing units will take on a personality. Some are friendly. Some are belligerent. Some are antagonistic. Some are smarter. Some, less so. The housing units take this personality from the strongest personality in the unit. So, if the strongest, most vocal personality is aggressive, the rest of the people in the unit will also behave more aggressively. If the strongest personality is pleasant, the rest of the people in the unit tend to behave the same way.

The "personality" this day, was aggressive and intent on showing that she was smarter than everyone else. Her demanding attitude and declaration that she would "learn nothing from this stupid book" infected several of the other women – including those who were on their bunks. Her attitude made everyone restless.

People who opt out of the class must lie on their bunks until I leave the unit. It always surprises me that people will choose not to take the class. The class is not difficult. People who take it get a pencil and an eraser – nothing to sneeze at when you're in prison. They also have the opportunity to sit and chat for a while and to learn new things. And, of course, they get the opportunity to earn a week's time off their sentence. It seems a much better choice than lying on one's bunk and keeping quiet for the session. For some reason, this particular unit had about ten people opt out of the class. Women in prison are not known for making the best choices.

My lead personality finally stopped bitching long enough for me to introduce myself and go around the table to learn the other women's names. When I got to her, her response was "why do you need to know my name?" I wasn't surprised, but I asked her to move to the end of the table and not to talk while we were going through the material. She complied.

Two women were interested in the material and engaged in the conversation. A third was shyer, but also interested. The fourth woman was initially quiet, until at one point she interrupted with an important declaration.

"They told me I'm too dangerous to get a job."

I told her that what we were talking about would be helpful in any situation. I asked the women if any had had jobs before they'd been incarcerated and if they wanted to go back to the same type of work or to try something new.

The shy woman told me she had been a dancer. I said that was really neat. Her cellmates laughed.

"She's a stripper," they said. I asked the woman if she was a good dancer – creative and coordinated. She said yes. I asked if she was used to dealing with paying customers who sometimes got difficult. She emphatically said yes. I said those were good job skills and that they were usable in other fields. She got less shy. Her cellmates stopped laughing.

By this time, I was feeling pretty good. My troublemaker was at the end of the table, taking notes. My shy lady was speaking up. My dangerous lady was listening. Maybe I was feeling too good about things.

Out of nowhere, my dangerous lady again declared that she was "way too dangerous to ever hold a job." I asked her how she planned to support herself.

"With SSI (Supplemental Security Income)," she said.

I asked if she had children.

"Yes." "Thirteen. My oldest is 19. She has two children. My twins are five months old."

"How do you plan to support them?"

"They have their own money," she said in a loud voice. "They get welfare, food stamps and cash cards. They're fine," she said getting agitated.

"Is that going to be good enough for them for the rest of their lives?" I asked.

At that point, the woman started yelling.

"Don't talk about my kids. Leave them alone. You got no right to talk about my kids."

She got up and stormed away from the table. She went to her bunk and kept yelling as I tried to go on with the class. I asked if she was leaving the class.

"Yes!"

She kept yelling at me and complaining to the other "bunkers". They started answering, in their own loud and aggressive voices. I

147

asked her to be quiet while she was on her bunk. She kept getting louder. Finally, she jumped off her bunk, went behind me into that forbidden space, and banged on the glass. She yelled to the deputies that she couldn't stay in the room because I had criticized her kids. The deputies took her out, and she sat with one in the hall for the rest of the class time.

A few minutes later, my dancer was called out by deputies. She started to cry as she picked up her box with her booking number on it. She kissed my first troublemaker good-bye and left with the deputies.

Left at the table were the two women who had been participating in the class all along, and the lead troublemaker, who by then was also participating. We finished our class and they did evaluations. All three evaluations said the class was very good and helpful. I felt like crying as I passed my "dangerous" woman on the way out.

*** 

I saw a lot of people who worked with prisoners take on the attitude of a strict kindergarten teacher. They purposefully used clear, firm directions and an insistence in tone and word choice that directives *would* be followed. I hated that. I thought I could just speak casually, respectfully, and in a friendly way to prisoners. Much of the time I could, but I had to always be on the alert. Some of those prisoners would start pushing the second they perceived weakness – even though I was really only being respectful. Many prisoners have a hard time telling the difference. Once one starts pushing, they all start pushing. That quickly becomes dangerous, and I had to constantly remind myself to never leave the opportunity for them to push.

The fact was, I still hated going to the prison. I hated being in a room of people who had been locked away from society and who had to do what others – almost always complete strangers – told them to do. I hated being a person who took on the role of bossing them around for the small amount of time I was with them.

So, why did I do it? I absolutely believe that if we're going to lock people away – and lots of people need to be locked away – then we have to help them figure a way out. We have to help them "pay their debt," and get on with their lives.

I believe jobs are the way to help people stay out of jail. There's an astronomically high recidivism rate for people who have been incarcerated. I believe jobs are the only way to lower that rate.

It's not easy getting a job when you have a felony conviction. It's a huge hurdle and most of the women are going to need a lot of help to jump it. If they don't get the help, if they don't get the job, they are not going to make it. They'll be right back in prison again.

I hate to see them there. I want them to be out, earning a salary and living their lives, rather than just marking time. I want them to be good moms. I want them to take care of their children – and to make sure that their children do not end up behind their own set of bars.

I questioned whether what I was doing would amount to a hill of beans. Would anyone get a job because I tried to help prepare her to look for one? I would never, ever know. I only knew that with odds against it, and with a very slim sliver of hope, some of them might. And that meant that no matter how depressed I got from my few hours a week in this most horrible place, I would keep going. Just in case something I said or did some day helped some of these ladies.

## February 21, 2019

I formally gave my notice that I will not be going back to the prison. I got no response from the deputy liaison. She is a nice lady, but like many at the jail, she doesn't really think that what I was trying to do would be very successful. Coming from a family of cops, I understand the opinion. They each shared it with me. But even as they recited recidivism rates and predicted a poor prognosis, they each encouraged me to try.

I felt badly that I wouldn't be going back, but I realized that my hatred of the prison, my hatred of locking people up, my hatred of the wasted lives, have all become more than I can tolerate on a regular basis. My weekly visits to the prison permeated every minute of my daily life. I'm embarrassed that I didn't try longer than nine months. My dread of penetrating those brick and concertina barricades, of passing through those iron bars, of being ever conscious that one camera or another was monitoring my every move, of sitting at those stainless-steel tables and bolted-down stools is only part of the reason I wouldn't go back. It was my sadness and misery that most of the women – I sometimes felt that it was all of the women – would not change their lives. It was my despair that nothing I did would ever change what they will do.

I thought my decision to stop going to the prison would disappoint the people around me, my husband, my family, friends, and supporters who encouraged me when I started working at the prison. I was surprised that they were all pretty relieved when I decided to stop. They saw how sad the work had made me, and they told me so.

My time at the prison was on my schedule. I could come and go at my choice. I didn't have to stay there, and I could make my own choices while I was there. During the time I worked at the prison, I kept feeling guilty that I dreaded the place so much, when I could leave whenever I wanted. The prisoners had to stay there until someone else said they could go.

And then it occurred to me. I hadn't done anything that caused society to put me in prison. Sadly, the incarcerated women had.

From the moment I first started training to work with women in prison, there were people who told me that I couldn't help the women. I didn't believe them. I believed that I could help them. I was wrong. But what I've also come to understand, is that there is a big difference between "they cannot be helped" and "I cannot help them."

Working with women in prison is not what I can do, but there are other ways I can make a difference. I'm still searching for the right fit.

And I'm still wishing a way out for those women who are locked in.

# The Piano Came Home

Carmela – January 30, 2018

Today I picked up my mother's piano.

It had been sitting at my brother-in-law's house in the Arizona desert for the previous five years. Before that it had moved from one person's house or storage shed to another since my mother died 18 years ago.

I grew up with that piano in the house although I never played it. I wanted to play it, but for one reason or another, I never took lessons.

I dusted and polished that piano about a million times growing up. I sat and picked at it now and again, but I never learned to play. Now in retirement – that part of life where we get to do everything we always wanted to do but never had time for – I have decided to learn to play.

I've been told by a woman who has made her living playing pianos and organs and even writing compositions, that I'm too old to learn – that I'll never play well. Williametta is a tiny, straight-forward old lady, who says what's on her mind.

"Well, I really want to learn," I told her. "My age means that I'll practice more and think more about it."

"That doesn't matter" she said, "you're too old to become very good."

"I don't really expect to be very good," I said. "Maybe just a little good."

"Nope. You're too old. You needed to start playing when you were 4 or 5 years old. Maybe even younger."

The conversation went on like that for several minutes, but how well I learn to play the piano really doesn't matter.

I go into it expecting that it will be hard, and that with my natural lack of rhythm, it'll be frustrating, and that I'll never be very good at all. But I want to make music, and so I made arrangements to get my mother's piano from its last home and to begin taking lessons.

Here's what I didn't expect. When I picked up the piano, it was dusty and scratched and sadly out of tune. George and I took it for a wild ride through the desert, where it broke free of its straps, rolled half-way across the 15-foot U Haul rental truck in which it rode alone, and somehow managed not to hit the sides or fall over.

We got it home and into the house. The keyboard cover wouldn't open without quite a lot of coaxing. But I coaxed, and it opened. Then I rubbed down the whole thing with orange oil and called a piano tuner.

And that's when my mother's piano suddenly became my piano. This piece of furniture that I had grown up with became something more than wood and strings and ivory keys. It became a living thing.

There's a relationship that humans get with instruments that make music that we don't get with other inanimate objects. I think it's because instruments give us music. They speak to us. They sing to us. And because they sing to us, the instruments become as precious as the sounds they make, as precious as the people who play them, and as precious as the people who listen to them. Pianos are forever capable of pulling up the memories and emotions that they first elicited.

I don't know how to play the piano on this day that I bring home my mother's piano. And, just as Williametta predicted, I'm sure I'll never be very good at it. But today, as I plunked those out-of-tune keys, I fell in love with the piano I grew up with.

And that's when my mother moved back home with me.

# The Man with a Bad Attitude

## George – October 14, 2019

I don't want to complain, but I've always marched to a different drummer. I recognized it even when I was a kid. Except back then, I would make an effort to get in step. It never worked.

Now, I don't even try.

It's a dangerous way to be nowadays, when society increasingly wants you to fit in, listen to what people in authority tell you, work together as a team, and reach a consensus with your peers.

Even when the consensus is bullshit, we're all supposed to pretend that it isn't.

Nowadays, more and more people are being sent to re-education camp to learn the proper way to think and the proper way to act. It's like when your mother wants to give you a lecture, and you'd rather just get a spanking and get it over with.

Re-education camp in the United States goes by such names as traffic school, sensitivity training, and forced apologies that folks are pressured to make whether they're actually sorry or not.

I used to go to traffic school when I got a ticket, just to keep my insurance rates within reason. Traffic school is a thing thought up by a bunch of bureaucrats to convince people to drive defensively. Having been to traffic school several times over the years, I can attest that everybody is just going through the motions – both the teachers and the students.

After they started offering traffic school online, I hired my young niece Bailey – nowhere near old enough to drive herself – to attend in my name and take the test. Over the months, she got pretty good at it.

If I do say so myself, I think I was instrumental in making her the fine driver that she is today.

Then there was an editor – long ago when I was a reporter at the Long Beach Press-Telegram – a rather stupid woman, whose name I cannot, and do not wish, to remember. She decided that the staff needed sensitivity training. Her idea was to teach reporters not to be mean to black, Hispanic, or Asian people.

Since I was no meaner to black, Hispanic, or Asian people than I was to anybody else, I didn't see the point.

The class was taught by a very nice black man, who showed us a film starring a little black boy, who came to a white neighborhood where people had big houses and spent their weekends at the country club. That certainly had not been my experience growing up white and poor, but that was the opening premise of the class – that white people spend their weekends at country clubs.

The instructor said, "if you don't think you need this class, then you are free to leave."

I left, much to the anger of the editor.

I have no idea where she is now, but I'm sure if she has not died of acute bitterness, she is somewhere, railing against how mean men are to women, white people are to black people, and Americans are to the rest of the world.

Then there was my pal, Roger, a very liberal and progressive kind of guy, with whom I got along despite our political differences. The problem was Roger thought if I didn't agree with him to the letter on every issue, that I obviously had a whole other set of "right-wing" values, whether I expressed them or not.

In Roger's mind, you are either this or you are that.

The end of my relationship with Roger came when he told me – using simple one-syllable words – that "what you need to understand George, is that: Black folks are good people. They are nice and they are fun."

I told him his statement was ridiculous.

Some black people are nice, fine folks and some are really jerks. The same as white people, brown people, Asians, and Indians.

That was the end of my relationship with Roger. It wasn't that he felt differently about things than I did, but that he insisted upon giving me a little lecture as though I was an idiot. And a bigot.

Time marches on.

Now, people are being forced – upon threat of losing their jobs or their status in society – to apologize for what they said or a joke that they told, no matter how long ago, and whether or not they are really sorry.

And some people, who declare they are not prejudiced, are being told they actually are, but they just don't know it. Women vote against what is good and right because their husbands make them do it. Or so the story goes.

The people who say this have obviously never met my wife, Carmela. If I dared to tell Carmela who to vote for, she would tell me in the most loving way possible, to mind my own damn business.

I like that about Carmela.

# Why are Experts Always so Wrong?

George – June 29, 2019

I don't trust experts. I never have, and I doubt that I ever will.

Experts are the guardians of the common wisdom. They are captives of the group-think of the day. That's the reason for which they go to school – to learn what they are supposed to believe. And most of them do exactly that.

When somebody tells me they have a PhD in Early Childhood Education, or Women's Studies, or Psychology, or Creative Dance, I am immediately suspicious of everything they have to say, even though much of it may be true.

What is the old joke? A "specialist" is someone who knows more and more about less and less until he knows everything about nothing.

I am also suspicious of people who went through elementary school, then high school, then college, and then they graduate and are officially anointed with a certificate of expert-hood, basically a piece of paper signed by some institute that charged them a lot of money and likely put them in debt.

The secondary school system was created more than a hundred years ago to prepare workers for factories. A bell rings and you change classes, another bell rings and you go to recess, another bell rings and you eat lunch. It doesn't matter if you are really excited about what you have just learned and want to hear more, when the bell rings you go on to the next assignment.

Today, it's still the same old shuck and jive – although the world has changed completely in the meantime.

As you might guess, I really hated school, and I wasn't too crazy about teachers.

And though at the end I was awarded a bachelor's degree, my time spent at the University was mostly a waste. The only thing that saved me from the nonsense taught at college was the perspective I gained working construction, as a party chief on a survey crew, fighting in a war, and living life.

When I completed my time at the University, I skipped the whole stupid cap and gown ceremony. I told them to send me my degree, and I split for California. I still have the degree and it's still in the little shipping tube in which it was mailed more than 50 years ago. To this day, I have never looked at it.

So why do I still have it, stored in a tube in the back of the closet? To remind me, always, of what a waste of my precious time it represents.

The point is that the overriding purpose of a formal education is to pigeonhole people into some kind of occupational box. I have talked to numerous successful people, who when pressed or drunk, would confess that what they really wanted to do was play the saxophone or create art or putter around in their garage inventing products that just might change the world.

It's those dreamers and the workers that push civilization forward, not the university-indoctrinated "experts."

At least that's the way I see it.

# Romance and Real Estate

### George – July 13, 2013

If you have ever been to West Texas, you know what I mean when I say it is one wide-open, oh-say-can-you-see piece of America. You can drive for mile after mile with nothing at all to obstruct the view of nothing at all.

Wilderness and desolation as far as the eye can see, with hardly any traffic on Interstate 10, and a posted speed limit of 80 mph, which means everybody is doing 85 or 90, except those brave folks who flash by in the triple digits.

And then, every once in a while, a sign. Like the one I spotted as I cruised by with Carmela on a brisk spring day – 20 acres, $16,000, and a phone number.

"Wow," I say to Carmela. "Twenty acres. $16,000. What do you think?"

"What do I think about what?" she asks.

"Buying some land, here in West Texas," I say, a little indignant at her tone.

"Look out the window. Wide-open spaces. No people, no trees, just jack rabbits, armadillos, coyotes, and buzzards to clean up the mess. This is God's country. It hasn't changed since the pioneers came across it in covered wagons."

"What would we do with a bunch of land out here in the middle of nowhere," she asks. Now I am a little offended because she just doesn't get it.

"Why, it would be our land," I say. "We would own it. We would walk around on it. We would wake up in the morning and gaze out at the vista and say THIS IS OUR LAND."

"Well, there it is," she says, gesturing out the window. "Pull over, get out, and walk around on it all you want for free. You can gaze at the vista and say THIS IS OUR LAND all you want, and nobody is going to care because nobody is going to hear you.

"And think about all the money we'll save by not actually buying it."

I shouldn't have been surprised, because I have always known that men are more romantic than women.

Sure, we may get up to go to the men's room or to get some popcorn at the movies when the shooting stops and the kissing begins, but it's not because we are not romantic. We just know that nothing important is going to happen in the next few minutes and this would be a good time to take a break.

The romantic part is when the cowboy straps on his guns and his sweetheart says, "please don't go, don't leave," and he just looks at her sadly and tells her how a man's got to do what a man's got to do. No matter how many times I see it or how many movies I see it in, that part still gets to me.

I'm thinking that buying a piece of land in West Texas is like that song by Ernest Ball and J. Keirn Brennan:

> We'll build a sweet little nest, somewhere in the West,
> And let the rest of the world go by.

I understand, we probably will not buy the property and build a sweet little nest, but what a nice thought. It's not reality; it's a romantic ideal, sort of like "I'd swim the widest ocean to be by your side." But that's not how my woman sees it.

She wants to know, do you think they have sewer hookups way out here or would we have to put in a septic tank? Where are we going to get our electricity? How are we going to take a bath with no running water? Where is the nearest grocery store? And what about zoning? You don't want somebody building a 24-hour Truck Stops of America or some kind of Indian gaming casino next to your "sweet little nest."

I was kind of sorry that I brought the whole subject up. Just then we get a call from our niece, who has actually been to West Texas. When she hears where we are, she talks about driving for hours through the scrub brush and rocks. West Texas, she decided on her last trip, would be a good place to bury a body.

She could have said what a nice place to plant a cactus garden or wouldn't it be fun to go rock hunting or bird watching there. No. Right away she goes to burying bodies.

This is the young woman whose feminist moment came in middle school when the teacher remarked that virtually all serial killers are men. Our niece immediately challenged him.

"What? You're saying women can't be serial killers?" she demanded. "Girls can do anything that boys can do. We could be serial killers, just as good as them."

Clearly a different perspective on the subject of men versus women and good versus evil, but not necessarily that far off the mark. My personal experience is that women can be every bit as vicious as men, but they usually find more elegant and devious ways of expressing their anger than going on murder sprees.

In fact, I concede that women are equal to men in almost every kind of occupational and recreational pursuit. But not romance. When it comes to true romance, women have little insight about how we men feel or what touches our hearts.

158

And I doubt they ever will.

**EPILOGUE:** Underneath that big Montana Sky. It's 2021, and Carmela has finally gotten some romance in her soul. We're still in the "let's pick a place on the map" stage, but some wide-open property with nothing more than butterflies, birds and bees and flowers and snakes on it seems to be in our future. Oh yeah, and a crazy old man, standing in the middle of it all yelling: THIS IS MY LAND!

# Chapter 4: Magical Times and Magical Places

**Preface:** There was this time more than 40 years ago when we were still getting to know each other and still hadn't said "I love you," when we took a ride out to the desert. We parked George's blue Mazda truck with the camper shell on the back in the Anza Borrego desert at a spot called Sand Canyon. Our plan was to sleep in the back of the truck, but the stars were so many and so high and so bright ... and then the Eagles came scratchy on the radio with:

> "I like the way your sparkling earrings lay,
> Against your skin so brown,
> And I want to sleep with you in the desert tonight,
> With a million stars all around..."

So instead of cuddling up in the camper, we lay on the floor of the desert and instead of sleeping, we spent the entire night just staring up at the stars. To this day, we both know "that night."

It was a magical night.

*Carmela*

# Essays

Making the Enchantment Last        164

A Sea of Flowers        166

Coming to Terms with the Past        167

Old Age        170

# Making the Enchantment Last

George - August 13, 2017

Thirty-two years ago, Carmela and I spent six weeks in Brazil – four of them in Rio de Janeiro and the other two traveling around that lovely land, visiting jungles and waterfalls, swamps and rivers, cities and countryside. It was more than beautiful. It was magical.

We never went back, I don't know why exactly. Maybe we feared the second time around it would be a lovely place, but not the magic place it had once been. Magic is elusive. It's not where you are, it's what is inside you at the time. You can go to the same place, see the same things, listen to the same lovely music, but the magic has slipped away.

The magic of that long-ago adventure remains in our memories and in our hearts.

There was that time we almost died in the ocean just a few hundred feet from the shops and high-rise apartments along Avenida Atlantica. We had been warned about the rip tides and currents that stalked the beach that time of year, but we were relying on the magic of the moment to protect us. And it did.

When the first huge breaker drove us under, then the second one swirled us upside down, and we were running out of air, I reached out, found Carmela's hand and pushed off from the sandy bottom.

We survived, clambered back ashore, went to our rented apartment, took a shower, and then went out to dinner. Another good day in Rio.

The ocean wasn't the only danger in Rio. We were warned again and again. Watch your back, don't wear any jewelry that can be snatched from your ears or jerked off your fingers, and don't think of resisting, especially if there is more than one robber.

And yet, we wandered where we chose, and the magic remained. Some of the most beautiful and exciting places on the planet are also the most dangerous. Such concerns can't defeat the magic of time or place.

Then there were the beggar kids, homeless boys who hustled money shining shoes. When they were young and still cute, they survived on handouts from tourists and even some sympathetic Cariocans, as the residents of Rio are known. But when they grew older, not so cute, and resentful of their lot in life, they often turned to crime.

There was one such boy we became attached to. He would greet us on the street and we would talk in a hodge-podge of broken English and fractured Portuguese. When we left, a few weeks later, he gave us one more shoeshine – refusing to take any money for it.

A token of our friendship. A little more magic.

If the world had been fair, we would have taken that kid home and made him part of our family. As it was, we thanked him, gave him a hug, and walked away.

After Rio, we traveled around that big, beautiful, wild country – to the Amazon and the Pantanal swamp wilderness, and to Iguazu Falls on the border of Brazil and Argentina.

We flew in and out of single runway airports that had been carved out of the jungle - loading and unloading passengers at every stop as though the plane was a city bus.

There were snakes and exotic birds. There were *capybara*, the world's largest rodent. Scores of jacaré, the Brazilian version of alligators, lined the river banks. Indian kids fished from the same bank. And of course, there were the legendary and deadly piranha that lurked beneath the surface.

We still think about going back sometimes, but would Rio and Brazil hold the same enchantment as it did on the trip so long ago. Probably not.

But what if it did?

# A Sea of Flowers

George – May 10, 2019

Carmela, Henry, and I went traveling last month to see the famous Southern California super bloom and experience a little history.

The super bloom doesn't happen every year, only when the state has experienced a lot of rain. And when that happens, the hillsides and valleys erupt with a full display of botanic beauty.

We've seen super blooms before, but to see this year's super bloom, we got in our car and drove 231 miles to the Carrizo Plain National Monument, a 250,000-acre preserve in the southeast corner of San Luis Obispo County near the Kern County line. There were spectacular flora displays closer to home, but my sweetheart and I longed for both the drive and the flowers.

The road we drove on that spring day was rough, unpaved for miles in some places with a great rocky and gravel washboard surface. But the weather was fantastic and the view unsurpassed. Carmela and I were spellbound by the natural beauty of the place. Henry followed Carmela down the trails and across the fields like a faithful little boy, pausing only to sniff the bushes and pee on the rocks. I took pictures and picked poppies.

It was a grand and glorious time.

# Coming to Terms with the Past
### George – November 9, 2016

Fifty-one years ago today, my life changed forever. There have been many changes since that time, some extremely good and some not so much, but I was one person before November 8, 1965 and another person afterwards.

I don't like to talk about it. I have tossed and turned through many sleepless nights, trying not to think about it, but now, more than half-a-century after that day, maybe it's time to write about some of my unresolved issues. For perspective, you can go on the internet and google "November 8, 1965, Vietnam."

It wasn't the bloodshed or the horror of war. By November 1965, I had seen quite enough of that. But the date marked the biggest Vietnam battle involving U.S. troops up to that time, although bigger and bloodier battles would come as the conflict dragged on. And I was wounded and medevacked early in the fight, so I was gone well before the worst of it.

The thing is, I knew it was going to happen days before it did. But I got it wrong. I was certain – positive – that I was going to die on the next mission. I even thought about writing a good-bye letter home, but what would I say?

167

*"Dear Mom.*
*I'm going to die in the next few days, please take care of my*
*little brothers.*
*Love George."*

And so I didn't write the letter, which was a good thing because I didn't die.

The platoon sergeant who was standing near me was killed, my radio operator who was standing next to me was killed, and the medic who was standing between me and the mortar round that exploded in our midst was killed. His body shielded me from much of the flying shrapnel. In fact, I was the last life he ever saved.

I'll skip the gory details, except to note that when Gen. William Tecumseh Sherman said "War is Hell" in 1870, he was not exaggerating.

I also will not reveal the names of my comrades who died that day, except to say that the platoon sergeant, who bled out on the floor of the helicopter during my ride back to a tent hospital, was a 34-year-old black man with a big smile and a kindness that belied his choice in careers.

The medic was a sweet-natured 19-year-old white kid, who dreamed of turning his Army job saving lives into a civilian pursuit after he was discharged.

My radio operator and I were from the weapons platoon. I was a forward observer, whose job was to call in mortar fire when the need arose. In the jungle, you usually couldn't see far enough through the underbrush to call in fire. During those times, I basically became just another guy with a gun. On November 8, 1965, I was three weeks shy of my 25th birthday.

To be honest, I was not particularly pleased with my radio operator. He was 18 years old, fresh out of some inner-city slum, with a bad attitude and a chip on his shoulder. He had been shot in the butt 34 days earlier, and the forward observer to whom he had been attached was killed. His was just a flesh wound, and it healed quickly, but it shook him to his core.

The sad truth was that he was a kid, and he was scared. He had the same premonition that I did – a premonition that he was going to die on the next mission. He had literally begged the weapons platoon sergeant not to make him go, but you don't get off the hook because you're scared. Everybody was scared. I was not particularly happy when he was assigned to me, but he got way worse than he deserved.

I mention race, only to note that it didn't seem to matter a whole lot on the battlefield. We were infantry. Our battalion was just about equally divided between black guys and white guys with a few Hispanics and other minorities mixed in. We didn't choose our friends by race. It wasn't exactly a warm and fuzzy love fest, but you knew who you could count on and trust and who you could not, and it had little to do with the color of anybody's skin.

When they finally got a helicopter to land in the middle of bullets flying through the trees, they loaded it so full, I had only a few inches of seat with my knees hanging out through the open doorway. Despite the noise of the engine and rotor, I remember the flight back as a quiet time. A couple of thousand feet above the jungle canopy with the doors open, the slip stream rushing past, it seemed cool and unreal as I went into shock. I am not religious – not then and not now – but I remember singing to myself all the hymns I learned going to the Baptist Church with my grandmother when I was barely 5.

The Old Rugged Cross, Bringing in the Sheaves, Peace in the Valley. And all the time I was wondering, why am I still here? Why am I alive when the others standing next to me are dead?

It would be nice to say that I saw the experience as a second chance, that I took control of the rest of my life and did something grand and good with it. Maybe I should have, but I did not. My experience was no more terrible or unique than thousands of other young men who fought in that mindless war and the terrible wars that followed.

Fifty-one years later, I'm doing pretty well. I have a woman who loves me, a couple of bucks in the bank, and a place to get out of the cold. I'm actually happy – maybe happier than I have ever been.

But the ghosts still come around on those sleepless nights, to stand sad and silent by my bed. Why you, they want to know. How come we died so young and you lived to be so old?

I have no answer, but I do think about them still. Especially on this day, 51 years later.

# Old Age

Today I turn 80. If life was a chess match, this would be the time to start moving in on the end game. But fuck that! Life is not a chess match. Life is an adventure. Balls out to the end.

That's my plan, and I'm sticking to it.

www.ingramcontent.com/pod-product-compliance
Lightning Source LLC
Chambersburg PA
CBHW060927040426
42445CB00011B/824